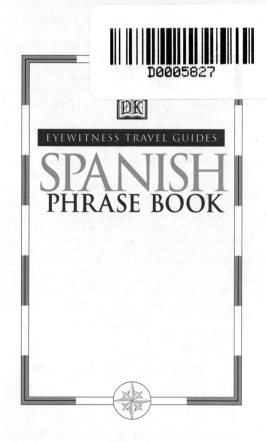

EYEWITNESS TRAVEL GUIDES

# SPANISH
## PHRASE BOOK

A Dorling Kindersley Book

LONDON, NEW YORK, MUNICH,
MELBOURNE, AND DELHI

Compiled by Lexus Ltd with
Alicia de Benito de Harland and Mike Harland

Published in the United States by DK Publishing, Inc.
375 Hudson Street, New York, NY 10014

First American Edition 1998
Reprinted with corrections 2000, 2003
10

Dorling Kindersley books can be purchased in bulk quantities at discounted
prices for use in promotions or as premiums. We are also able to offer special
editions and personalized jackets, corporate imprints, and excerpts from all of
our books, tailored specifically to meet your own needs. To find out more, please
contact: Special Markets Department, Dorling Kindersley Publishing, Inc.,
375 Hudson Street, New York, NY 10014; Fax: 212-689-5254.

Library of Congress Cataloging-in-Publication Data
Spanish phrase book. -- 1st American ed.
     p.    cm. -- (Dorling Kindersley travel guide phrase books)
English and Spanish.
Includes index.
ISBN–13: 978–0–7894–9493–1
1. Spanish language--Conversation and phrase books--
English.  I. DK Publishing. Inc.  II. Series.
PC4121.S6765  1998
468.3′421--DC21                   97–47228
                                     CIP

Printed and bound in China by Leo Paper Products Limited

see our complete catalog at
**www.dk.com**

# CONTENTS

# PREFACE

This *Dorling Kindersley Eyewitness Travel Guides Phrase Book* has been compiled by experts to meet the general needs of tourists and business travelers. Arranged under headings such as Hotels, Driving, and so forth, the ample selection of useful words and phrases is supported by a 2,000-line mini-dictionary. There is also an extensive menu guide listing approximately 600 dishes or methods of cooking and presentation.

Typical replies to questions you may ask during your trip, and the signs or instructions you may see or hear, are shown in tinted boxes. In the main text, the pronunciation of Spanish words and phrases is imitated in English sound syllables. The Introduction provides guidelines to Spanish pronunciation.

*Dorling Kindersley Eyewitness Travel Guides* are recognized as the world's best travel guides. Each title features specially commissioned color photographs, detailed maps, cutaways of major buildings and 3-D aerial views, plus information on sights, events, hotels, restaurants, shopping, and entertainment.

*Dorling Kindersley Eyewitness Travel Guides* titles include:
Spain · Barcelona · Madrid · Seville & Andalusia · Amsterdam
Australia · Sydney · Berlin · Budapest · California · Florida
Hawaii · New York · San Francisco & Northern California · Canada
France · Loire Valley · Paris · Provence · Great Britain · London
Ireland · Dublin · Scotland · Greece: Athens & the Mainland
The Greek Islands · Istanbul · Italy · Florence & Tuscany
Milan & the Lakes · Naples · Rome · Sardinia · Sicily
Venice & the Veneto · Jerusalem & the Holy Land · Mexico
Moscow · St Petersburg · Portugal · Lisbon · Prague
South Africa · Thailand · Vienna · Warsaw

# INTRODUCTION

## PRONUNCIATION

When reading the imitated pronunciation, stress the part that is underlined. Pronounce each syllable as if it formed part of an English word and you will be understood sufficiently well. Remember the points below and your pronunciation will be even closer to the correct Spanish.

| | |
|---|---|
| g | always hard as in "get" |
| H | represents the guttural sound of "ch" |
| I | pronounced as "eye" |
| ow | as in "cow" |
| s | always sound the Spanish "s" as a double "ss" as in "missing," *never* like the "s" in "easy" |
| th | as in "thin," *not* as in "they" |
| y | always as in "yet," *not* as in "eye" (e.g. **bien** *byen*, **siento** *syentoh*) |

Don't be worried by the varying pronunciations you are certain to hear in some parts of Spain. An example is the sounding of "z" (and of "c" before e or i) like an English "s"—in this instance we recommend that you don't copy it, but lisp the sound as we have imitated it. Similarly, in certain circumstances, the Spanish "v" can be pronounced as either a "v" or a "b," so that **vaca** sounds like "baca."

## GENDERS AND ARTICLES

Spanish has two genders for nouns—masculine and feminine. In this book, we generally give the definite article ("the")—**el** for masculine nouns, **la** for feminine nouns, **los** for masculine plural nouns, and **las** for feminine plural nouns. Where the indefinite article ("a, an") is more appropriate, we have given **un** for masculine nouns and **una** for feminine nouns, or the words for "some"—**unos** (masculine) and **unas** (feminine).

# USEFUL EVERYDAY PHRASES

## Yes, No, OK, etc.

**Yes/No**
Sí/No
*see/noh*

**Excellent!**
¡Estupendo!
*estoopendoh*

**Don't!**
¡No!
*noh*

**OK**
Vale
*baleh*

**That's fine**
Está bien
*esta byen*

**That's right**
Eso es
*essoh ess*

## Greetings, Introductions

**How do you do? Pleased to meet you**
¿Qué tal?, mucho gusto
*keh tal, mootchoh goostoh*

**Good morning/good evening/good night**
Buenos días/buenas tardes/buenas noches
*bweh-noss dee-ass/bweh-nass tardess/bweh-nass notchess*

**Goodbye/Bye**
Adiós
*ad-yoss*

**How are you?** *(familiar)*
¿Cómo está usted?       ¿Cómo estás?
*koh-moh esta oosteh*       *koh-moh estass*

**My name is …**
Me llamo …
*meh yah-moh*

**What's your name?** *(familiar)*
¿Cómo se llama usted?       ¿Cómo te llamas?
*koh-moh seh yah-ma oosteh*       *koh-moh teh yah-mass*

**What's his/her name?**
¿Cómo se llama él/ella?
*koh-moh seh yah-ma el/eh-ya*

**May I introduce …?**
Le presento a …
*leh presentoh a*

**This is …** *(introducing a man/woman)*
Éste/ésta es …
*esteh/esta ess*

**Hello/Hi!**
¡Hola!
*oh-la*

**See you later!**
¡Hasta luego!
*asta lweh-goh*

**It's been nice meeting you** *(to a man/woman)*
Mucho gusto en conocerle/conocerla
*mootchoh goostoh en konoh-thairleh/konoh-thairla*

## PLEASE, THANK YOU, APOLOGIES

**Thank you/No, thank you**
Gracias/No, gracias
*grath-yass/noh grath-yass*

**Please**
Por favor
*por fa-vor*

**Excuse me!** *(when sneezing, etc.)*
¡Perdón!
*pair-don*

**Sorry!**
¡Perdón!/Lo siento
*pair-don/loh syentoh*

**I'm really sorry**
Lo siento muchísimo
*loh syentoh mootchee-seemoh*

**It was/wasn't my fault**
Ha sido/no ha sido culpa mía
*a seedoh/noh a seedoh koolpa mee-a*

## WHERE, HOW, ASKING

**Excuse me, please** *(to get past)*
¿Me hace el favor?
*meh ah-theh el fa-vor*

**Can you tell me ...?**
¿Puede decirme ...?
*pweh-deh detheer-meh*

**Can I have ...?**
¿Me da ...?
*meh da*

**Would you like a …?**
¿Quiere un/una …?
*kyeh-reh oon/oona*

*(familiar)*
¿Quieres un/una …?

**Would you like to …?**
¿Le gustaría …?
*leh goostaree-a*

*(familiar)*
¿Te gustaría …?

**Is there … here?**
¿Hay … aquí?
*I … akee*

**What's that?**
¿Qué es eso?
*keh ess esso*

**Where can I get …?**
¿Dónde puedo conseguir …?
*dondeh pweh-doh konseh-geer*

**How much is it?**
¿Cuánto es?
*kwantoh ess*

**Where is the …?**
¿Dónde está el/la …?
*dondeh esta el/la*

**Where are the restrooms?**
¿Dónde están los servicios?
*dondeh estan loss sair-veeth-yoss*

**Is there wheelchair access?**
¿Hay acceso para sillas de ruedas?
*I akthesoh a parra seeyahs de rooedas*

**Are there facilities for the disabled?**
¿Hay acceso a minusváli dos?
*I akthesoh a meenoosvalee dos*

## About Oneself

**I'm from …**
Soy de …
*soy deh*

**I'm … years old**
Tengo … años
*teng-goh … ahn-yoss*

**I'm a …**
Soy …
*soy*

**I'm married/divorced**
Estoy casado/divorciado
*estoy kasadoh/deevorss-yah-doh*

**I'm single**
Soy soltero
*soy soltairoh*

**I have … sisters/brothers/children**
Tengo … hermanas/hermanos/hijos
*teng-goh … airmah-nass/airmah-noss/ee-Hoss*

## Likes, Dislikes, Socializing

**I like/love …**
Me gusta/encanta el/la …
*meh goosta/enkanta el/la*

**I like/love swimming/traveling**
Me gusta/encanta nadar/viajar
*meh goosta/enkanta nadar/vya-Har*

**I don't like …**
No me gusta el/la …
*noh meh goosta el/la*

**I don't like swimming/traveling**
No me gusta nadar/viajar
*noh meh goosta nadar/vya-нar*

**I hate …**
Detesto …
*detestoh*

**Do you like …?**
¿Le gusta …?
*leh goosta*

**It's delicious/awful!**
¡Es delicioso/horrible!
*ess deleeth-yohsoh/orreebleh*

**I don't drink/smoke**
No bebo/fumo
*noh beboh/foomoh*

**Do you mind if I smoke?**
¿Le importa que fume?
*leh eemporta keh foomeh*

**I don't eat meat or fish**
No como carne ni pescado
*noh koh-moh karneh nee peskadoh*

**What would you like (to drink)?**
¿Qué quiere (beber/tomar)?
*keh kyeh-reh bebair/tomar*

**I would like a …**
Quería …
*keh-ree-a*

**Nothing for me, thanks**
No quiero nada, gracias
*noh kyeh-roh nada grath-yass*

**I'll get this one**
Ahora invito yo
*a-ora eembeetoh yoh*

**Cheers!** *(toast)*
¡Salud!
*saloo*

**I would like to …**
Quería …
*keh-ree-a*

**Let's go to Seville/the movies**
Vamos a Sevilla/al cine
*vamoss a sevee-ya/al theeneh*

**Let's go swimming/for a walk**
Vamos a nadar/a dar un paseo
*vamoss a nadar/a dar oon passeh-oh*

**What's the weather like?**
¿Qué tiempo hace?
*keh tyempoh ah-theh*

**The weather's awful**
Hace un tiempo malísimo
*ah-theh oon tyempoh maleesseemoh*

**It's pouring down**
Está lloviendo a cántaros
*esta yovyendoh a kant-ah-ross*

**It's really hot**
Hace muchísimo calor
*ah-theh mootcheesseemoh kalor*

## HELP, PROBLEMS

**Can you help me?**
¿Puede ayudarme?
*pweh-deh ayoodarmeh*

**I don't understand**
No comprendo
*noh komprendoh*

**Do you speak English/French/German/?**
¿Habla usted inglés/francés/alemán?
*ah-bla oosteh eengless/franthess/alleh-man*

**Does anyone here speak English?**
¿Hay alguien aquí que hable inglés?
*i algyen akee keh ahbleh eengless*

**I can't speak Spanish**
No hablo español
*noh ah-bloh esspan-yoll*

**I don't know**
No sé
*noh seh*

**What's wrong?**
¿Qué pasa?
*keh passa*

**Please speak more slowly**
Por favor, hable más despacio
*por fa-vor ah-bleh mass desspath-yoh*

**Please write it down for me**
Por favor, escríbamelo
*por fa-vor eskreeba-meh-loh*

**I've lost my way**
Me he perdido
*meh eh pairdeedoh*

**Go away!**
¡Váyase!
*vah-ya-seh*

## TALKING TO RECEPTIONISTS, ETC.

**I have an appointment with …**
Tengo una cita con …
*teng-goh oona theeta kon*

**I'd like to see …**
Quisiera ver a …
*keess-yeh-ra vair a*

**Here's my card**
Aquí tiene mi tarjeta
*akee tyeneh mee tar-Heh-ta*

**My company is …**
Soy de la compañía …
*soy deh la kompanyee-a*

**May I use your phone?**
¿Puedo usar su teléfono?
*pweh-doh oossar soo teh-leffonoh*

---

### THINGS YOU'LL HEAR

| | |
|---|---|
| ¡adelante! | come in! |
| aquí tiene | here you are |
| ¡bien! | good! |
| ¡buen viaje! | have a good trip! |
| ¿cómo? | excuse me? |
| ¿cómo está usted? | how are you? |

→

| | |
|---|---|
| ¿cómo le va? | how are things? |
| ¡cuánto lo siento! | I'm so sorry! |
| ¡cuidado! | look out! |
| de acuerdo | OK |
| de nada | you're welcome, don't mention it |
| ¿de verdad? | is that right? |
| ¡encantado! | pleased to meet you! |
| eso es | that's right |
| exactamente/exacto | exactly |
| gracias, igualmente | thank you, the same to you |
| ¡hasta luego! | goodbye! see you later! |
| ¡hola! | hello! hi! |
| muchas gracias | thank you very much |
| muy bien, gracias —¿y usted? | very well, thank you —and you? |
| no comprendo | I don't understand |
| no sé | I don't know |
| por favor | please |
| ¿qué ha dicho? | what did you say? |
| ¿qué tal?, mucho gusto | how do you do? nice to meet you |
| sírvase usted mismo | help yourself |

## THINGS YOU'LL SEE

| | |
|---|---|
| abierto | open |
| agua potable | drinking water |
| ascensor | elevator |
| aseos | restrooms |
| caballeros | men |
| caja | cashier, checkout, cash register |
| calle | street |
| carretera | road |
| cerrado (por vacaciones) | closed (for vacation period) |

→

| | |
|---|---|
| día festivo | national holiday |
| empujar | push |
| entrada | entrance |
| entrada gratuita/libre | admission free |
| entre sin llamar | enter without knocking |
| festivos | official holidays |
| horas de oficina | opening times |
| horas de visita | visiting hours |
| información turística | tourist information |
| laborables | working days |
| lavabos | restroom |
| ocupado | occupied |
| peligro | danger |
| planta baja | ground floor |
| precaución | caution |
| primer piso | second floor |
| privado | private |
| prohibido | prohibited, forbidden |
| recién pintado | wet paint |
| reservado | reserved |
| salida | exit |
| salida de emergencia | emergency exit |
| se alquila piso | apartment for rent |
| segundo piso | third floor |
| señoras | women's restroom |
| se prohíbe la entrada | no admittance |
| servicios | restroom |
| se vende | for sale |
| silencio | silence, quiet |
| sótano | basement |
| tirar | pull |

# COLLOQUIALISMS

*You may hear these: to use some of them yourself could be risky!*

| | |
|---|---|
| emborra charse | to get drunk |
| a mares | a lot |
| ¡anda ya! | get away! come off it! |
| cabrón | S.O.B. |
| cacharro | thing |
| ¡cierra el pico! | shut your mouth! |
| ¡no me vengas con esas! | you're kidding me! |
| de pacotilla | trashy |
| ¡Dios mío! | my God! |
| ¡me encanta qué maravilla! | that's really terrific! |
| ¡estupendo! | wonderful! |
| ¡genial! | great! fantastic! |
| ha sido una putada | it was a pain/nuisance |
| imbécil | imbecile |
| ir de copas | to go drinking |
| la mar de … | really/very … |
| lo digo de cachondeo | I'm only joking |
| ¡maldita sea! | damn! |
| me está tomando el pelo | you're pulling my leg |
| ¡ni de coña! | no way! |
| ¡no me da la (real) gana! | I'm damned if I will! |
| putada | *(a general expression of annoyance)* |
| ¡qué barbaridad! | no way! |
| ¿qué hay? | how's things? |
| ¡qué va! | no way! |
| tía | girl |
| tío | guy |
| ¡vaya por Dios! | oh, dear! |
| ¡váyase a paseo! | get lost! |
| ¡vete a hacer puñetas! | get away! |
| ya está | there you are |

# DAYS, MONTHS, SEASONS

| | | |
|---|---|---|
| Sunday | domingo | *dom<u>ee</u>ngoh* |
| Monday | lunes | *l<u>oo</u>ness* |
| Tuesday | martes | *m<u>a</u>rtess* |
| Wednesday | miércoles | *my<u>a</u>irkoh-less* |
| Thursday | jueves | *Hw<u>eh</u>-vess* |
| Friday | viernes | *vy<u>ai</u>rness* |
| Saturday | sábado | *s<u>a</u>bbadoh* |
| | | |
| January | enero | *enn<u>eh</u>-roh* |
| February | febrero | *febr<u>eh</u>-roh* |
| March | marzo | *m<u>a</u>rthoh* |
| April | abril | *abr<u>ee</u>l* |
| May | mayo | *m<u>a</u>yyoh* |
| June | junio | *H<u>oo</u>n-yoh* |
| July | julio | *H<u>oo</u>l-yoh* |
| August | agosto | *ag<u>o</u>stoh* |
| September | septiembre | *set-y<u>e</u>mbreh* |
| October | octubre | *okt<u>oo</u>breh* |
| November | noviembre | *nov-y<u>e</u>mbreh* |
| December | diciembre | *deeth-y<u>e</u>mbreh* |
| | | |
| Spring | primavera | *preema-v<u>eh</u>-ra* |
| Summer | verano | *ver<u>a</u>h-noh* |
| Fall | otoño | *ot<u>o</u>n-yoh* |
| Winter | invierno | *eemb-y<u>a</u>irnoh* |
| | | |
| Christmas | Navidad | *navee-d<u>a</u>* |
| Christmas Eve | Nochebuena | *notcheh-bw<u>eh</u>-na* |
| Easter | Pascua, | *p<u>a</u>skwa,* |
| | Semana Santa | *sem<u>a</u>h-na s<u>a</u>nta* |
| Good Friday | Viernes Santo | *vy<u>a</u>irness s<u>a</u>ntoh* |
| New Year | Año Nuevo | *<u>a</u>hn-yoh nw<u>eh</u>-voh* |
| New Year's Eve | Nochevieja | *notcheh-vy<u>eh</u>-Ha* |

# NUMBERS

| | | | |
|---|---|---|---|
| 0 | cero *theh-roh* | 10 | diez *dyeth* |
| 1 | uno, una* *oonoh, oona* | 11 | once *ontheh* |
| 2 | dos *doss* | 12 | doce *doh-theh* |
| 3 | tres *tress* | 13 | trece *treh-theh* |
| 4 | cuatro *kwatroh* | 14 | catorce *katortheh* |
| 5 | cinco *theenkoh* | 15 | quince *keentheh* |
| 6 | seis *sayss* | 16 | dieciséis *dyeth-ee-sayss* |
| 7 | siete *see-eh-teh* | 17 | diecisiete *dyeth-ee-see-eh-teh* |
| 8 | ocho *otchoh* | 18 | dieciocho *dyeth-ee-otchoh* |
| 9 | nueve *nweh-veh* | 19 | diecinueve *dyeth-ee-nweh-veh* |

20  veinte *vaynteh*
21  veintiuno *vayntee-oonoh*
22  veintidós *vayntee-doss*
30  treinta *traynta*
31  treinta y uno *traynti oonoh*
32  treinta y dos *traynti doss*
40  cuarenta *kwarenta*
50  cincuenta *theen-kwenta*
60  sesenta *sessenta*
70  setenta *setenta*
80  ochenta *otchenta*
90  noventa *noh-venta*
100  cien *thyen*
110  ciento diez *thyentoh dyeth*
200  doscientos, doscientas *doss-thyentoss, doss-thyentass*
500  quinientos, quinientas *keen-yentoss, keen-yentass*
700  setecientos, setecientas *seh-teh-thyentoss, seh-teh-thyentass*
1,000  mil *meel*
1,000,000  un millón *mee-yon*

* When **uno** precedes a masculine noun, it loses the final o,
e.g. "1 point" is **un punto**. Feminine nouns take **una**, e.g.
"1 bag," **una bolsa**. Numbers in the hundreds, 200, 300, etc.,
use the form ending in **-as** with feminine nouns, e.g. "300
notes," **trescientos billetes**; " 300 weeks," **trescientas semanas**.

# TIME

| today | hoy | *oy* |
|---|---|---|
| yesterday | ayer | *ayyair* |
| tomorrow | mañana | *man-yah-na* |
| the day before yesterday | anteayer | *anteh-ayyair* |
| the day after tomorrow | pasado mañana | *passah-doh man-yah-na* |
| this week | esta semana | *esta semah-na* |
| next week | la semana que viene | *la semah-na keh vyeh-neh* |
| this morning | esta mañana | *esta man-yah-na* |
| this afternoon | esta tarde | *esta tardeh* |
| this evening | esta tarde/noche | *esta tardeh/notcheh* |
| tonight | esta noche | *esta notcheh* |
| yesterday afternoon | ayer por la tarde | *ayyair por la tardeh* |
| last night | anoche | *annotcheh* |
| tomorrow morning | mañana por la mañana | *man-yah-na por la man-yah-na* |
| tomorrow night | mañana por la noche | *man-yah-na por la notcheh* |
| in three days | dentro de tres días | *dentroh deh tress dee-ass* |
| three days ago | hace tres días | *ah-theh tress dee-ass* |
| late | tarde | *tardeh* |
| early | temprano | *temprah-noh* |
| soon | pronto | *prontoh* |
| later on | más tarde | *mass tardeh* |
| at the moment | en este momento | *en esteh momentoh* |
| second | un segundo | *segoondoh* |
| minute | un minuto | *meenootoh* |
| quarter of an hour | un cuarto de hora | *kwartoh deh ora* |
| half an hour | media hora | *meh-dya ora* |
| three quarters of an hour | tres cuartos de hora | *tress kwartoss deh ora* |

| hour | la hora | _ora_ |
|---|---|---|
| day | el día | _dee-a_ |
| every day | todos los días | _todoss loss dee-ass_ |
| all day | todo el día | _todoh el dee-a_ |
| the next day | al día siguiente | _al dee-a seegyenteh_ |
| week | la semana | _semah-na_ |
| month | el mes | _mess_ |
| year | el año | _ahn-yoh_ |

## TELLING TIME

The 24-hour clock is used in Spain, both in the written form (as in timetables) and verbally (e.g. in inquiry offices). However, you will still hear the 12-hour clock used in everyday life.

"O'clock" is not normally translated in Spanish unless it is for emphasis, when **en punto** would be used. For example: (**es**) **la una** (**en punto**) is "(it's) one o'clock." The plural form of the verb is used for all other hours, e.g. (**son**) **las cinco** (**en punto**) is "(it's) five o'clock."

The word "past" is translated as **y** (= "and"). In order to express minutes after the hour, state the hour followed by **y** plus the number of minutes: so **las seis y diez** is "ten past six." The word "to" is translated as **menos** (= "less"). So, for example, **las diez menos veinte** is "twenty to ten." The word for "quarter" is **cuarto**; **las siete menos cuarto** is "quarter to seven" and **las cinco y cuarto** is "quarter past five." The half hour is expressed using **y media**, so **las seis y media** is "6:30."

The word "at" is translated as **a** followed by **las**. For example, **a las tres y cuarto** is "at quarter past three." Remember to change **las** to **la** when using "one," thus "at 1:30" becomes **a la una y media**.

The expressions "AM" and "PM" have no direct equivalents, but the expressions **de la mañana** (in the morning), **de la tarde** (in the afternoon/evening—which extends up to 8 PM in Spain), and **de la noche** (at night—i.e. from 8 PM) are used to distinguish between times that might otherwise be confusing.

For example, "6 AM" is **las seis de la mañana** and "6 PM" is **las seis de la tarde**; "10 AM" is **las diez de la mañana** and "10 PM" is **las diez de la noche**.

| **what time is it?** | ¿qué hora es? | *keh ora ess* |
|---|---|---|
| AM | de la mañana | *deh la man-yah-na* |
| **PM** *(up to 8 PM)* | de la tarde | *deh la tardeh* |
| *(from 8 PM)* | de la noche | *deh la notcheh* |
| **one o'clock** | la una | *la oona* |
| **ten past one** | la una y diez | *la oona ee dyeth* |
| **quarter past one** | la una y cuarto | *la oona ee kwartoh* |
| **1:30** | la una y media | *la oona ee meh-dya* |
| **twenty to two** | las dos menos veinte | *lass doss meh-noss vaynteh* |
| **quarter to two** | las dos menos cuarto | *lass doss meh-noss kwartoh* |
| **two o'clock** | las dos (en punto) | *lass doss (en poontoh)* |
| **13:00** | las trece horas | *lass treh-theh orass* |
| **16:30** | las dieciséis treinta | *lass dyeth-ee-sayss traynta* |
| **20:10** | las veinte diez | *lass vaynteh dyeth* |
| **at seven o'clock** | a las siete | *a lass see-eh-teh* |
| **noon** | mediodía | *meh-dyoh dee-a* |
| **midnight** | medianoche | *meh-dya notcheh* |

## THE CALENDAR

The cardinal numbers on page 19 are used to express the date in Spanish. However, sometimes in formal Spanish, the ordinal number may be used instead, but only to express "the first":

| **May first** | el uno/el primero de mayo | *el oonoh/el preemeh-roh deh mayyoh* |
|---|---|---|
| **June twentieth** | el veinte de junio | *el vaynteh deh Hoon-yoh* |

# HOTELS

Hotels are divided into five classes (with star ratings), followed by the **pensiones** (guesthouses), which have three. Farther down the scale come the **hotel residencia** for longer stays and the **hostal**, which is similar to a **pensión**. **Casas Rurales** are country houses whose owners accept visitors. The previously state-run **paradores** are superior (often converted castles, palaces, etc.) and allow unlimited stays, although you will have to pay for the extra comfort and scenery. If traveling in peak season, it is always advisable to reserve accommodations in advance in the more popular areas.

## USEFUL WORDS AND PHRASES

| | | |
|---|---|---|
| **balcony** | el balcón | *bal-kon* |
| **bath (tub)** | la bañera | *ban-yeh-ra* |
| **bathroom** | el cuarto de baño | *kwartoh deh bahn-yoh* |
| **bed** | la cama | *kah-ma* |
| **bed and breakfast** | alojamiento y desayuno | *aloh-Hamyentoh ee dessa-yoonoh* |
| **bedroom** | la habitación | *abbee-tath-yon* |
| **bill** | la cuenta | *kwenta* |
| **breakfast** | el desayuno | *dessa-yoonoh* |
| **dining room** | el comedor | *kommeh-dor* |
| **dinner** | la cena | *theh-na* |
| **double bed** | la cama doble, la cama de matrimonio | *kah-ma doh-bleh, kah-ma deh matreemonyoh* |
| **double room** | una habitación doble | *abbee-tath-yon doh-bleh* |
| **elevator** | el ascensor | *ass-then-sor* |
| **foyer** | el hall | *Hol* |
| **full board** | pensión completa | *penss-yon kompleh-ta* |
| **guesthouse** | la pensión | *penss-yon* |
| **half board** | media pensión | *meh-dya penss-yon* |
| **hotel** | el hotel | *oh-tell* |
| **key** | la llave | *yah-veh* |
| **lounge** | el salón | *sa-lon* |

23

| | | |
|---|---|---|
| lunch | la comida | *komee-da* |
| maid | la camarera | *kamareh-ra* |
| manager | el director | *deerek-tor* |
| parking lot | el aparcamiento | *aparkamyentoh* |
| receipt | la factura | *fak-toora* |
| reception | la recepción | *reh-thepth-yon* |
| receptionist | el recepcionista | *reh-thepth-yoneesta* |
| restroom | los servicios | *vattair, retreh-teh* |
| room | la habitación | *abbee-tath-yon* |
| room service | el servicio de | *sairveeth-yoh deh* |
| | habitaciones | *abbeetath-yoh-ness* |
| shower | la ducha | *dootcha* |
| single bed | la cama individual | *kah-ma eendeeveed-wal* |
| single room | una habitación | *abbee-tath-yon* |
| | individual | *eendeeveed-wal* |
| sink | el lavabo | *lavah-boh* |
| twin room | una habitación | *abbee-tath-yon kon* |
| | con dos camas | *doss kah-mass* |

**Do you have any vacancies?**
¿Tienen alguna habitación libre?
*tyeh-nen algoona abbee-tath-yon leebreh*

**I have a reservation**
He hecho una reserva
*eh etchoh oona reh-sairva*

**I'd like a single room**
Quería una habitación individual
*keh-ree-a oona abbee-tath-yon eendeeveed-wal*

**I'd like a room with a balcony/bathroom**
Quería una habitación con balcón/cuarto de baño
*keh-ree-a oona abbee-tath-yon kon bal-kon/kwartoh deh bahn-yoh*

**Is there satellite/cable TV in the rooms?**
¿Hay televisión por satélite/por cable en las habitaciones?
*i televeesseeon por sateleete/por kable en las abbee-tath-yoh-ness*

**I'd like a room for one night/three nights**
Quería una habitación para una noche/para tres noches
*keh-ree-a oona abbee-tath-yon parra oona notcheh/parra tress notchess*

**What is the charge per night?**
¿Cuál es la tarifa por noche?
*kwal ess la tarreefa por notcheh*

**I don't yet know how long I'll stay**
Todavía no sé cuánto tiempo me voy a quedar
*todavee-a noh seh kwantoh tyempoh meh voy a keh-dar*

**When is breakfast/dinner?**
¿A qué hora es el desayuno/la cena?
*a keh ora ess el dessa-yoonoh/la theh-na*

**Please wake me at … o'clock**
Haga el favor de llamarme a las …
*ah-ga el fa-vor deh yamar-meh a lass*

**May I have breakfast in my room?**
¿Pueden servirme el desayuno en mi habitación?
*pweh-den sair-veermeh el dessa-yoonoh en mee abbee-tath-yon*

**I'd like to have some laundry done**
Quisiera utilizar el servicio de lavado
*keess-yeh-ra ooteeleethar el sairveeth-yoh deh lavah-doh*

**I'll be back at … o'clock**
Volveré a las …
*volveh-reh a lass*

**My room number is …**
El número de mi habitación es el …
*el noomeh-roh deh mee abbee-tath-yon ess el*

**My reservation was for a double room**
Había reservado una habitación doble
*abee-a resairvah-doh oona abbee-tath-yon doh-bleh*

**I asked for a room with private bathroom**
Pedí una habitación con baño
*peh-dee oona abbee-tath-yon kon bahn-yoh*

**The lamp is broken**
La lámpara está rota
*la lampara esta rohta*

**There is no toilet paper in the bathroom**
No hay papel higiénico en el cuarto de baño
*noh I papel ee-Hyeneekoh en el kwartoh deh bahn-yoh*

**The window won't open**
No se puede abrir la ventana
*noh seh pweh-deh abreer la ventah-na*

**There isn't any hot water**
No hay agua caliente
*noh I ahg-wa kalyenteh*

**The outlet in the bathroom doesn't work**
El enchufe del cuarto de baño no funciona
*el entchoofeh del kwartoh deh bahn-yoh noh foonthyoh-na*

**I'm leaving tomorrow**
Me marcho mañana
*meh martchoh man-yah-na*

**When do I have to vacate the room?**
¿A qué hora tengo que desocupar la habitación?
*a keh ora teng-goh keh dessokoopar la abbee-tath-yon*

**Can I have the bill, please?**
¿Me da la cuenta, por favor?
*meh da la kwenta por fa-vor*

**I'll pay by credit card**
Pagaré con tarjeta (de crédito)
*pagareh kon tar-Heh-ta deh kredeetoh*

**I'll pay cash**
Pagaré al contado
*pagareh al kontahdoh*

**Can you get me a taxi?**
¿Puede llamar a un taxi?
*pweh-deh yamar a oon taksee*

**Can you recommend another hotel?**
¿Puede recomendarme otro hotel?
*pweh-deh rekomendarmeh otroh oh-tell*

## Things You'll See

| | |
|---|---|
| acceso prohibido | staff only |
| albergue | country hotel |
| almuerzo | lunch |
| alojamiento y desayuno | bed and breakfast |
| aparcamiento | parking, parking lot |
| ascensor | elevator |
| baño | bath |
| cena | dinner |
| CH | boardinghouse |
| comedor | dining room |
| comida | lunch, meal |
| completo | no vacancies |
| cuarto de baño | bathroom |
| cuenta | bill |
| desayuno | breakfast |
| empujar | push |
| entrada | entrance |
| escaleras | stairs |
| hotel-residencia | residential hotel |
| HR | residential hotel |
| media pensión | half board |
| parador | luxury hotel |

→

| | |
|---|---|
| pensión | guesthouse |
| pensión completa | full board |
| planta baja | ground floor |
| primer piso | second floor |
| prohibida la entrada | no admission |
| prohibido el paso | staff only |
| salida de emergencia | emergency exit |
| salón | lounge |
| servicio | restroom |
| solo para residentes | hotel patrons only |
| tirar | pull |
| WC | restroom |

## THINGS YOU'LL HEAR

**Lo siento, está lleno**
I'm sorry, we're full

**El hotel está completo**
We don't have any vacancies

**No nos quedan habitaciones individuales/dobles**
There are no single/double rooms left

**¿Para cuántas noches?**
For how many nights?

**¿Va a pagar al contado, o con tarjeta?**
Will you be paying by cash or credit card?

**Haga el favor de pagar por adelantado**
Please pay in advance

**Tiene que desocupar la habitación antes de las doce**
You must vacate the room by noon

# CAMPING AND TRAILER TRAVEL

There are plenty of recognized sites all over Spain, especially along the Mediterranean coast, and most are open all year round. At other sites, you will need a permit from landowners or authorities such as the Forestry Authority. Ask the Spanish Tourist Office for details.

Youth hostels are open to members of the YHA, but in the peak season it is best to make a reservation in advance and stays are limited to three nights. You can get details from the Spanish Tourist Office in New York or local offices in Spain.

## USEFUL WORDS AND PHRASES

| backpack | la mochila | *motcheela* |
|---|---|---|
| bucket | el cubo | *koo-boh* |
| camper (RV) | la caravana | *karavah-na* |
| camper site | un camping | *kampeen* |
| campfire | una hoguera | *oh-geh-ra* |
| campsite | un camping | *kampeen* |
| go camping | ir de camping | *eer deh kampeen* |
| cooking utensils | los utensilios de cocina | *ootenseel-yoss deh kotheena* |
| drinking water | agua potable | *ahg-wa pottah-bleh* |
| garbage | la basura | *bassoora* |
| groundcloth | la lona impermeable | *loh-na eempair-meh-ah-bleh* |
| hitchhike | hacer auto-stop | *athair owtoh-stop* |
| rope | una cuerda | *kwairda* |
| saucepans | las cazuelas | *kath-weh-lass* |
| sleeping bag | el saco de dormir | *sah-koh deh dormeer* |
| tent | la tienda | *tyenda* |
| youth hostel | el albergue juvenil | *albairgeh Hooveneel* |

**Can I camp here?**
¿Puedo acampar aquí?
*pweh-doh akampar akee*

**Can we park the camper here?**
¿Podemos aparcar aquí la caravana?
*podeh-moss apar-kar akee la karavah na*

**Where is the nearest campsite/camper site?**
¿Dónde está el camping más cercano?
*dondeh esta el kampeen mass thair-kah-noh*

**What is the charge per night?**
¿Cuál es la tarifa por noche?
*kwal ess la tarreefa por notcheh*

**How much is it for a week?**
¿Cuánto es para una semana?
*kwantoh ess parra oona sehmah-na*

**I only want to stay for one night**
Es sólo para una noche
*ess soh-loh parra oona notcheh*

**We're leaving tomorrow**
Nos vamos mañana
*noss vah-moss manyah-na*

**Where is the kitchen?**
¿Dónde está la cocina?
*dondeh esta la kotheena*

**Can I light a fire here?**
¿Puedo encender fuego aquí?
*pweh-doh enthen-dair fweh-goh akee*

**Where can I get …?**
¿Dónde puedo conseguir …?
*dondeh pweh-doh konseh-geer*

**Is there any drinking water?**
¿Hay agua potable aquí?
*I ahg-wa pottah-bleh akee*

## THINGS YOU'LL SEE

| | |
|---|---|
| agua | water |
| agua potable | drinking water |
| albergue juvenil | youth hostel |
| aseos | restroom |
| camping | campsite, camper site |
| cocina | kitchen |
| duchas | showers |
| fuego | fire |
| luz | light |
| manta | blanket |
| no se admiten perros | no dogs allowed |
| precio | price |
| prohibido … | no … |
| prohibido acampar | no camping |
| prohibido el paso | no trespassing |
| prohibido encender fuego | no campfires |
| saco de dormir | sleeping bag |
| se alquila | for rent |
| se prohíbe … | … forbidden |
| supermercado | supermarket |
| tarifa | charges |
| tienda | store |
| uso | use |
| WC | restroom |

# VILLAS AND APARTMENTS

You may be asked to pay for certain "extras" not included in the original price. You might want to ask if electricity, gas, etc., is included. It's a good idea to ask about an inventory of household goods at the beginning, rather than be told something is missing just as you are about to leave. You may be asked for a deposit, so make sure you get a receipt for it.

## USEFUL WORDS AND PHRASES

| | | |
|---|---|---|
| agency | la agencia | ah-Henthya |
| bath (tub) | el baño | bahn-yoh |
| bathroom | el cuarto de baño | kwartoh deh bahn-yoh |
| bedroom | el dormitorio | dormee-tor-yoh |
| blind | la persiana | perss-yahna |
| blocked | atascado | atass-kah-doh |
| boiler | la caldera | kaldeh-ra |
| break | romper | rompair |
| broken | roto | rohtoh |
| caretaker | el encargado, | enkargah-doh, |
| | el portero | porteh-roh |
| central heating | la calefacción central | kaleffakthyon thentral |
| cleaner | la señora de la | sen-yora deh la |
| | limpieza | leempyeh-tha |
| comforter | el edredón | edreh-don |
| deposit | el depósito | deh-posseetoh |
| drain | el desagüe | desahg-weh |
| electrician | un electricista | elektreeth̲eesta |
| electricity | la electricidad | elektreetheedad |
| faucet | un grifo | greefoh |
| fusebox | la caja de fusibles | kah-Ha deh foosseebless |
| gas | el gas | gas |
| garbage can | (el cubo de) la basura | kooboh deh la bassoora |
| grill | la parrilla, el grill | parree-ya, greell |
| heater | la estufa | estoofa |
| iron | la plancha | plantcha |

| | | |
|---|---|---|
| **ironing board** | la tabla de planchar | *tah-bla deh plantchar* |
| **key(s)** | la(s) llave(s) | *la(ss) yahveh(ss)* |
| **kitchen** | la cocina | *kotheena* |
| **leak** (*in roof*) | una gotera | *gohteh-ra* |
| (*in pipe*) | un agujero | *ahgoo-Heh-roh* |
| **light** | la luz | *looth* |
| **light bulb** | la bombilla | *bombee-ya* |
| **living room** | el cuarto de estar | *kwartoh deh estar* |
| **maid** | la sirvienta | *seervyenta* |
| **pillow** | la almohada | *almoh-ahda* |
| **pillowcase** | la funda de almohada | *foonda deh almoh-ahda* |
| **plumber** | un fontanero, | *fontaneh-roh,* |
| | plomero | *plomeh-roh* |
| **refrigerator** | la nevera | *neh-veh-ra* |
| **refund** | un reembolso | *reh-embolsoh* |
| **sheets** | las sábanas | *sahbanass* |
| **shower** | la ducha | *dootcha* |
| **sink** | el fregadero | *fregadeh-roh* |
| **stopper** | la llave de paso | *yah-veh deh pah-soh* |
| **stove** | la cocina | *kotheena* |
| **swimming pool** | la piscina | *peessthee-na* |
| **swimming pool technician** | el encargado de la piscina | *enkargah-doh deh la peessthee-na* |
| **toilet** | el retrete, el wáter | *retreh-teh, vattair* |
| **towel** | la toalla | *toh-ay-a* |
| **washing machine** | la lavadora | *lavadora* |
| **water** | el agua | *ahg-wa* |
| **water heater** | el calentador (del agua) | *kalentador del ahg-wa* |

**Does the price include electricity/cleaning?**
¿Está la electricidad/la limpieza incluída?
*esta la elektreetheedad/la leempyeh-tha eenklweeda*

**Do I need to sign an inventory?**
¿Hará falta que firme algún inventario?
*ara falta keh feermeh algoon eembentaryoh*

**Where is this item?**
¿Dónde está este artículo?
*dondeh esta esteh arteekooloh*

**Please take it off the inventory**
Haga el favor de quitarlo del inventario
*ah-ga el fa-vor deh keetarloh del eembentaryoh*

**We've broken this**
Se nos ha roto esto
*seh noss a rohtoh estoh*

**This was broken when we arrived**
Esto estaba roto cuando llegamos
*estoh estah-ba rohtoh kwandoh yehgah-moss*

**This was missing when we arrived**
Esto faltaba cuando llegamos
*estoh faltah-ba kwandoh yehgah-moss*

**Can I have my deposit back?**
¿Me devuelve el depósito?
*meh deh-vwelveh el deh-posseetoh*

**Can we have an extra bed?**
¿Puede ponernos otra cama más?
*pweh-deh ponairnoss otra kah-ma mass*

**Can we have more dishes/cutlery?**
¿Puede ponernos más platos y vasos/cubiertos?
*pweh-deh ponairnoss mass plah-toss ee vah-soss/koob-yairtoss*

**Where is …?**
¿Dónde está …?
*dondeh esta*

**When does the maid come?**
¿Cuándo viene la sirvienta?
*kwandoh vyeh-neh la seervyenta*

**Where can I buy/find …?**
¿Dónde podría comprar/encontrar …?
*dondeh podree-a komprar/enkontrar*

**How does the water heater work?**
¿Cómo funciona el calentador (de agua)?
*koh-moh foonthyoh-na el kalentador deh ahg-wa*

**Do you do baby-sitting?**
¿Hace usted de canguro?
*ah-theh oosteh deh kan-goo-roh*

**Do you make lunch/dinner?**
¿Prepara usted la comida/la cena?
*prepah-ra oosteh la komee-da/la theh-na*

**Do we have to pay extra or is it included?**
¿Hay que pagar aparte o está incluído en el precio?
*I keh pagar aparteh oh esta eenklweedoh en el prethyoh*

**The shower doesn't work**
No funciona la ducha
*noh foonthyoh-na la dootcha*

**The sink is blocked**
El fregadero está atascado
*el fregadeh-roh esta ataskah-doh*

**The sink/toilet is leaking**
Sale agua del fregadero/retrete
*sah-leh ahg-wa del fregadeh-roh/retreh-teh*

**There's a burst pipe**
Hay una cañería rota
*I oona kan-yeree-a rohta*

**The roof leaks**
Hay una gotera en el tejado
*I oona gohteh-ra en el teh-Hah-doh*

**The tank leaks**
Hay un agujero en el depósito
*I oon ahgoo-Heh-roh en el deposseetoh*

**There's a gas leak**
El gas se está saliendo
*el gas seh esta salyendoh*

**The garbage has not been collected for three days**
Llevan tres días sin recoger la basura
*yeh-van tress dee-ass seen rekoh-Hair la bassoora*

**There's no electricity/gas/water**
No hay luz/gas/agua
*noh I looth/gas/ahg-wa*

**The bottled gas has run out—how do we get a new canister?**
Se ha acabado el butano—¿cómo podemos conseguir otra
bombona?
*seh ah akabah-doh el bootah-noh—koh-moh podeh-moss konsegeer
oh-tra bomboh-na*

**Can you fix it today?**
¿Puede arreglarlo hoy?
*pweh-deh arreglarlo oy*

**Send your bill to …**
Mande la factura a …
*mandeh la faktoora a*

**I'm staying at …**
Estoy en …
*estoy en*

**Thanks for looking after us so well**
Gracias por tratarnos tan bien
*grath-yass por tratarnoss tam byen*

**See you again next year**
Hasta el año que viene
*asta el ahn-yoh keh vyeh-neh*

# DRIVING

Spanish highways (**autopistas**) can be expensive to use because of the tolls. The best roads to use are the national main roads (**nacionales**). They often have passing lanes for heavy vehicles, especially on gradients. In recent years, however, many divided highways (**autovías**) have been built. However, secondary roads, **comarcales**, may be in quite poor condition.

The rule of the road is drive on the right, pass on the left. Secondary roads yield to major routes at intersections. In the case of roads having equal status, or at unmarked intersections, traffic coming from the **RIGHT** has priority. Look for the pictorial signs for priority on narrow bridges, etc. A system worth noting for changing direction or for crossing over divided highways is a semicircular exit ramp that is usually noted by **cambio de sentido**.

The speed limit on the **autovías** is 62 mph (100 km/h), and on the **autopistas** it's 75 mph (120 km/h). On **nacionales** it's 56 mph (90 km/h). In built-up areas the limit will vary between 25–35 mph (40—60 km/h).

Equipment to be carried at all times includes a spare set of light bulbs and a red triangle in case of breakdown or an accident. The traffic police patrols, **Guardia Civil de Tráfico**, will help you if you're in trouble, just as they will be ready to fine you on the spot should you break the law! Gas stations on the main roads are usually open 24 hours a day. They are seldom self-service. Unleaded gas is not readily available outside cities and main tourist areas. Fuel ratings are as follows: **extra** leaded, **gas-oil** diesel, **sin plomo** unleaded.

Parking in Spain is generally not restrictive—look for the signs, since there aren't any markings on the curb. In main towns and cities, however, the central area will come under what is often known as the **zona azul**, with only restricted parking allowed. Look for parking meters or the more common "pay and display" points. There are more and more underground parking lots, too, that operate on a ticket and barrier system.

## Some Common Road Signs

| | |
|---|---|
| aduana | customs |
| apagar luces de cruce | headlights off |
| aparcamiento | parking lot |
| atención al tren | beware of trains |
| autopista | highway |
| autovía | divided highway |
| callejón sin salida | no thoroughfare |
| calle peatonal | pedestrians only |
| calzada deteriorada | bad surface |
| calzada irregular | uneven surface |
| cambio de sentido | intersection |
| carretera cortada | road closed |
| ceda el paso | yield |
| centro ciudad | city center |
| centro urbano | town center |
| circule despacio | slow |
| circunvalación | circular road |
| cruce | intersection |
| desvío | detour |
| desvío provisional | temporary detour |
| encender luces de cruce | headlights on |
| escalón lateral | no hard shoulder |
| escuela | school |
| final de autopista | end of highway |
| firme en mal estado | bad surface |
| hielo | black ice |
| información turística | tourist information |
| obras | road construction |
| ojo al tren | beware of trains |
| paso a nivel | train crossing |
| paso subterráneo | pedestrian underpass |
| peaje | toll |
| peatón, circule a la izquierda | pedestrians, keep to the left |

→

| | |
|---|---|
| **peatones** | pedestrians |
| **peligro** | danger |
| **peligro deslizamientos** | slippery road surface |
| **precaución** | caution |
| **prohibido aparcar** | no parking |
| **prohibido el paso** | no trespassing |
| **puesto de socorro** | first-aid station |
| **salida de camiones** | construction exit |
| **vado permanente** | in constant use *(no parking)* |
| **vehículos pesados** | heavy vehicles |
| **velocidad controlada por radar** | automatic speed monitor |
| **zona azul** | restricted parking zone |
| **zona de estacionamiento limitado** | restricted parking area |

## USEFUL WORDS AND PHRASES

| | | |
|---|---|---|
| **automatic** | automático | *owtoh-m<u>a</u>teekoh* |
| **brake** | el freno | *fr<u>eh</u>-noh* |
| **breakdown** | una avería | *avveh-r<u>ee</u>-a* |
| **car** | el coche | *k<u>o</u>tcheh* |
| **clutch** | el embrague | *embr<u>ah</u>-geh* |
| **divided highway** | la autovía | *owtoh-v<u>ee</u>-a* |
| **drive** | conducir | *kondoo-th<u>ee</u>r* |
| **driver's license** | el permiso/el carnet de conducir | *pairm<u>ee</u>sso/karn<u>eh</u> deh kondoo-th<u>ee</u>r* |
| **engine** | el motor | *moh-t<u>or</u>* |
| **exhaust** | el tubo de escape | *t<u>oo</u>boh deh esk<u>ah</u>-peh* |
| **fanbelt** | la correa del ventilador | *korr<u>eh</u>-a del venteela-d<u>or</u>* |
| **garage** *(for repairs)* | un taller | *tayair* |
| **gas** | la gasolina | *gassoh-l<u>ee</u>na* |
| **gas station** | una gasolinera | *gassoh-leen<u>eh</u>-ra* |
| **gear** | la marcha | *m<u>a</u>rtcha* |
| **gears** | las marchas | *m<u>a</u>r-tchass* |
| **headlights** | las luces de cruce | *l<u>oo</u>thess deh kr<u>oo</u>-theh* |

| | | |
|---|---|---|
| **highway** | la autopista | owtoh-_peesta_ |
| **hood** | el capó | kap_o_ |
| **intersection** | el cruce | kr_oo_-theh |
| **junction** | el cruce | kr_oo_-theh |
| (*highway entry*) | un enlace de entrada | enl_ah_-theh deh entr_ah_-da |
| (*highway exit*) | un enlace de salida | enl_ah_-theh deh sal_ee_da |
| **license plate** | la matrícula | matr_ee_-koola |
| **manual** | manual | man-w_a_l |
| **mirror** | el (espejo) retroviso | esspeh-Hoh retroh-vessor |
| **motorcycle** | la moto (cicleta) | motoh-thee-kl_eh_-ta |
| **parking lot** | el aparcamiento | aparkam_y_entoh |
| **road** | la carretera | karreh-t_eh_-ra |
| **spare parts** | los repuestos | reh-pw_e_stoss |
| **spark plug** | la bujía | boo-H_ee_-a |
| **speed** | la velocidad | velothee-d_a_ |
| **speed limit** | el límite de velocidad | _l_eemeeth deh velothee-d_a_ |
| **speedometer** | el cuentakilómetros | kwenta-keel_o_meh-tross |
| **steering wheel** | el volante | voh-l_a_nteh |
| **taillights** | las luces traseras | _l_oothess-trass_eh_-rass |
| **tire** | el neumático | neh-oo-m_a_teekoh |
| **tow** | remolcar | reh-molk_a_r |
| **trailer** | la caravana | karra-v_ah_-na |
| **transmission** | la caja de velocidades | k_ah_-ha deh velotheed_ah_-dess |
| **traffic lights** | el semáforo | seh-m_a_fforoh |
| **trailer** | el remolque | reh-m_o_lkeh |
| **truck** | el camión | kam-y_o_n |
| **trunk** | el maletero | malleh-t_eh_-roh |
| **turn signal** | intermitente | eentairmeet_e_nteh |
| **van** | la furgoneta | foorgon_eh_-ta |
| **wheel** | la rueda | rw_eh_-da |
| **windshield** | el parabrisas | para-br_ee_-sass |
| **windshield wiper** | el limpiaparabrisas | _l_eempya-parabr_ee_ssass |

**I'd like some gas/oil/water**
Quería gasolina/aceite/agua
*keh-ree-a gassoh-leena/athay-teh/ahg-wa*

**Fill it up, please!**
¡Lleno, por favor!
*yeh-noh por fa-vor*

**35 liters of leaded gas, please**
Póngame treinta y cinco litros de extra
*ponga-meh traynti theenkoh leetross deh extra*

**Would you check the tires, please?**
¿Podría revisar los neumáticos, por favor?
*podree-a revee-sarmeh loss neh-oo-muteekoss por fa-vor*

**Do you do repairs?**
¿Hacen reparaciones?
*ah-then reparrath-yoh-ness*

**Can you repair the clutch?**
¿Pueden arreglarme el embrague?
*pweh-den arreh-glarmeh el embrah-geh*

**There is something wrong with the engine**
Hay algo que no va bien en el motor
*I algoh keh noh va byen en el moh-tor*

**The engine is overheating**
El motor se calienta demasiado
*el moh-tor seh kal-yenta deh-massyah-doh*

**I need a new tire**
Necesito un neumático nuevo
*neh-thessee-toh oon neh-oo-matikoh nweh-voh*

**Can you replace this?**
¿Pueden cambiarme esto?
*pwehden kambyarmeh estoh*

**The turn signal is not working**
El intermitente no funciona
*el eentairmeetenteh noh foonthyoh na*

**How long will it take?**
¿Cuánto tiempo tardarán?
*kwantoh tyempoh tardaran*

**I'd like to rent a car**
Quería alquilar un coche
*keh-ree-a alkee-lar oon kotcheh*

**I'd like an automatic/a manual**
Quiero un coche automático/manual
*kyeroh oon kotcheh owtoh-mateekoh/man-wal*

**How much is it for one day?**
¿Cuánto cuesta para un día?
*kwantoh kwesta parra oon dee-a*

**Is there a mileage charge?**
¿Tiene suplemento por kilómetro?
*tyeh-neh sooplementoh por keelometroh*

**When do I have to return it?**
¿Cuándo tengo que devolverlo?
*kwandoh teng-goh keh devolvairloh*

**Where is the nearest garage?**
¿Dónde está el taller más cercano?
*dondeh esta el tayair mass thair-kah-noh*

**Where is the nearest gas station?**
¿Dónde está la gasolinera más cercana?
*dondeh esta la gassoh-leeneh-ra mass thair-kah-na*

**Where can I park?**
¿Dónde puedo aparcar?
*dondeh pweh-doh appar-kar*

**Can I park here?**
¿Puedo aparcar aquí?
*pweh-doh appar-kar akee*

**How do I get to Seville?**
¿Cómo se va a Sevilla?
*koh-moh seh va a sevee-ya*

**Is this the road to Malaga?**
¿Es ésta la carretera de Málaga?
*ess esta la karreh-teh-ra deh malaga*

**Which is the quickest way to Madrid?**
¿Cuál es el camino más rápido para Madrid?
*kwal ess el kameenoh mass rapeedoh parra madreed*

---

### DIRECTIONS YOU MAY BE GIVEN

| | |
|---|---|
| a la derecha/izquierda | on the right/left |
| después de pasar el/la … | go past the … |
| la primera a la derecha | first on the right |
| la segunda a la izquierda | second on the left |
| todo recto | straight ahead |
| tuerza a la derecha | turn right |
| tuerza a la izquierda | turn left |

---

### THINGS YOU'LL SEE

| | |
|---|---|
| aceite | oil |
| agua | water |
| aire | air |
| apague el motor | turn off engine |
| aparcamiento subterráneo | underground parking lot |
| área de servicios | service area, highway services |
| cola | line (of cars) |

→

43

| completo | parking lot full |
| entrada | entrance |
| estación de servicio | service station |
| extra | leaded |
| garaje | garage |
| gas-oil | diesel |
| gasolina | gas, fuel |
| gasolinera | gas station |
| introduzca el dinero exacto | exact change |
| nivel del aceite | oil level |
| presión | air pressure |
| presión de los neumáticos | tire pressure |
| prohibido fumar | no smoking |
| recoja su ticket | take a ticket |
| reparación | repairs |
| salida | exit |
| sin plomo | unleaded |
| solo para residentes del hotel | hotel guests only |
| taller (de reparaciones) | garage (for repairs) |
| (tren de) lavado automático | car wash |

## THINGS YOU'LL HEAR

**¿Lo quiere automático o manual?**
Would you like an automatic or a manual?

**Su permiso/carnet de conducir, por favor**
May I see your driver's license?

**Su pasaporte, por favor**
Your passport, please

# TRAVELING AROUND

## Air Travel

Numerous international airlines provide services to Spanish destinations including Madrid, Barcelona, Bilbao, Valencia, Alicante, Malaga, Seville, Santiago, Tenerife, and Las Palmas in the Canaries, and Palma, Menorca, and Ibiza in the Balearic Islands. There is also a domestic network connecting the main cities in Spain.

## Train Travel

The Spanish national railroad system is called **RENFE** (*ren-fay*). Most trains are slow when compared to long-distance buses, even between major cities, but they are reasonably comfortable and inexpensive. The main types of trains are:

| | |
|---|---|
| AVE | High-speed train covering the Madrid–Seville line. |
| TALGO and TER | Fast diesel trains with air conditioning; you pay a supplement in addition to the normal fare. The **TALGO** is much more luxurious than the **TER**. |
| TAF | Slower diesel train used on secondary routes. |
| Exprés | A misleading name, since this is a slow night train stopping at all stations. |
| Rápido | Also misleading since it is just a daytime version of the **Exprés**. |
| Automotor Cercanías Ferrobús Omnibús | Local short-distance trains. |

## Long-Distance Bus Travel

There is an excellent bus network covering all of Spain, giving a better connecting service between cities than, and covering the gaps in, the railroad system. The buses are comfortable and fast, and have facilities such as video and air conditioning.

## LOCAL BUSES

All Spanish cities have a good bus system. Most buses are one-person operated and you pay the driver as you enter. Since there is generally a flat fare, it is less expensive to buy a book of tickets called a **bonobús**. There are also other types of tickets.

## SUBWAY

Madrid, Barcelona, Valencia, and Bilbao have a subway system, the **metro**. You can pick up information about tickets and prices at stations and tourist information centers.

## BOAT AND TAXI

There is a daily boat service to the Balearics (usually overnight) and a less frequent service to the Canaries, taking about two days. There is also a daily ferry linking Algeciras to North African ports such as Tangiers, Ceuta, and Melilla.

Taxis display a green light at night, and a sign on the windshield says if they are available (**libre**).

## USEFUL WORDS AND PHRASES

| adult | un adulto | *adool-toh* |
|-------|-----------|-------------|
| airport | el aeropuerto | *ah-airoh-pwair-toh* |
| airport bus | el autobús del aeropuerto | *owtoh-booss del ah-airoh-pwair-toh* |
| aisle seat | un asiento de pasillo | *ass-yentoh deh passee-yoh* |
| baggage claim | la recogida de equipajes | *rekoh-Heeda deh ekee-pah-hess* |
| boarding pass | la tarjeta de embarque | *tar-Heh-ta deh embar-keh* |
| boat | el barco billetes | *barkoh bee-yeh-tess* |
| buffet | la cafetería | *kaffeh-teh-ree-a* |
| bus | el autobús | *owtoh-booss* |
| bus station | la estación de autobuses | *estath-yon deh owtoh-boossess* |
| bus stop | la parada del autobús | *parah-da del owtoh-booss* |

| | | |
|---|---|---|
| car *(train)* | el vagón | *va-gon* |
| check in desk | el mostrador de | *mostra-dor deh* |
| | facturación | *faktoorath-yon* |
| child | un niño/una niña | *neen-yoh/neen-yah* |
| compartment | el compartimento | *kompartee-mentoh* |
| connection | un enlace | *enlah-theh* |
| cruise | un crucero | *krootheh-roh* |
| currency | el cambio de | *kamb-yoh deh* |
| exchange | moneda | *monneh-da* |
| customs | aduana | *ad-wah-na* |
| departure lounge | salidas | *salee-dass* |
| dining car | el vagón-restaurante | *va-gon restow-ranteh* |
| dock | el muelle | *mweh-yeh* |
| domestic | nacional | *nath-yonal* |
| driver | el conductor | *kondook-tor* |
| emergency exit | la salida de | *salee-da deh eh-mair-* |
| | emergencia | *Henth-ya* |
| entrance | la entrada | *entrah-da* |
| exit | la salida | *salee-da* |
| fare | el billete | *bee-yeh-teh* |
| ferry | el ferry | *ferree* |
| first class | primera (clase) | *preemeh-ra klah-seh* |
| flight | el vuelo | *vweh-loh* |
| flight number | el número de vuelo | *noomeh-roh deh vweh-loh* |
| gate | la puerta | *pwair-ta* |
| | (de embarque) | *deh embar-keh* |
| international | internacional | *eentairnath-yonal* |
| lost and found | la oficina de objetos | *offee-theena deh ob-Heh-* |
| | perdidos | *toss pairdee-doss* |
| luggage cart | un carrito para | *karree-toh parra el* |
| | el equipaje | *ekee-pah-Heh* |
| luggage storage | la consigna | *konseeg-na* |
| office | | |
| nonsmoking | no fumadores | *noh fooma-doress* |
| number 5 bus | el (autobús número) | *owtoh-booss noomeh-* |
| | cinco | *roh theenkoh* |

| | | |
|---|---|---|
| **one-way ticket** | un billete de ida | *bee-yeh-teh deh eeda* |
| **passport** | el pasaporte | *passa-porteh* |
| **platform** | el andén | *an-den* |
| **port** | el puerto | *pwair-toh* |
| **railroad** | el ferrocarril | *ferroh-karreel* |
| **reservation office** | el despacho de | *dess-patchoh deh* |
| **reserved seat** | un asiento reservado | *ass-yentoh reh-sair-vah-doh* |
| **round-trip ticket** | un billete de ida y vuelta | *bee-yeh-teh deh eeda ee vwel-ta* |
| **seat** | un asiento | *ass-yentoh* |
| **second class** | segunda (clase) | *segoonda klah-seh* |
| **sleeper car** | el coche-cama | *kotcheh kah-ma* |
| **station** | la estación | *estath-yon* |
| **subway** | el metro | *meh-troh* |
| **taxi** | un taxi | *taksee* |
| **terminal** (*bus*) | la terminal | *tairmee-nal* |
| (*subway*) | la estación terminal | *estath-yon tairmee-nal* |
| **ticket** | un billete | *bee-yeh-teh* |
| **timetable** | el horario | *oh-rar-yoh* |
| **train** | el tren | *tren* |
| **transit system map** | un plano | *plah-noh* |
| **underground passage** | paso subterráneo | *passoh soob-terrah-neh-oh* |
| **waiting room** | la sala de espera | *sah-la deh espeh-ra* |
| **window seat** | un asiento de ventanilla | *ass-yentoh deh ventanee-ya* |

## Air Travel

### A nonsmoking seat, please
Un asiento en la sección de no fumadores, por favor
*oon ass-yentoh en la sekth-yon deh noh fooma-doress por fa-vor*

### I'd like a window seat, please
Quería un asiento junto a la ventanilla, por favor
*keh-ree-a oon ass-yentoh Hoontoh a la ventanee-ya por fa-vor*

**How long will the flight be delayed?**
¿Cuánto retraso lleva el vuelo?
*kwantoh reh-trah-soh yeh-va el vweh-loh*

**Which gate for the flight to ...?**
¿Cuál es la puerta de embarque para el vuelo de ...?
*kwal ess la pwair-ta deh embar-keh parra el vweh-loh deh*

## TRAIN, BUS, AND SUBWAY TRAVEL

**When does the train/bus for Cadiz leave?**
¿A qué hora sale el tren/autobús para Cádiz?
*a keh ora sah-leh el tren/owtoh-booss parra kah-deeth*

**When does the train/bus from Barcelona arrive?**
¿A qué hora llega el tren/autobús de Barcelona?
*a keh ora yeh-ga el tren/owtoh-booss deh bartheh-loh-na*

**When is the next train/bus to Alicante?**
¿A qué hora sale el próximo tren/autobús para Alicante?
*a keh ora sah-leh el prok-seemoh tren/owtoh-booss parra aleekanteh*

**When is the first/last train/bus to Saragossa?**
¿A qué hora sale el primer/último tren/autobús para Zaragoza?
*a keh ora sah-leh el preemair/ool-teemoh tren/owtoh-booss parra
  tharagoh-tha*

**What is the fare to Granada?**
¿Cuánto cuesta el billete para Granada?
*kwantoh kwesta el bee-yeh-teh parra granahda*

**Do I have to pay a supplement?**
¿Tengo que pagar suplemento?
*teng-goh keh pagar soopleh-mentoh*

**Do I have to change?**
¿Tengo que hacer transbordo?
*teng-goh keh athair tranz-bordoh*

**Does the train/bus stop at Salamanca?**
¿Para el tren/autobús en Salamanca?
*pah-ra el tren/owtoh-booss en salamanka*

**How long does it take to get to Cordoba?**
¿Cuánto tiempo se tarda en llegar a Córdoba?
*kwantoh tyempoh seh tar-da en yeh-gar a kordohba*

**Where can I buy a ticket?**
¿Dónde puedo sacar un billete?
*dondeh pweh-doh sakar oon bee-yeh-teh*

**A one-way/round-trip ticket to Gerona, please**
Un billete de ida/de ida y vuelta a Gerona, por favor
*oon bee-yeh-teh deh eeda/deh eeda ee vwel-ta a Herrohna por fa-vor*

**Is there a discount for children?**
¿Hay precios especiales para niños?
*i pretheeos espethyales parra neen-yoss*

**Could you help me get a ticket?**
¿Podría usted ayudarme a sacar un billete?
*podree-a oosteh ayoo-darmeh a sakar oon bee-yeh-teh*

---

### Replies You May Be Given

**El próximo tren sale a las dieciocho horas**
The next train leaves at 18:00

**Haga transbordo en Salamanca**
Change at Salamanca

**Tiene que pagar suplemento**
You must pay a supplement

**Ya no quedan asientos para Madrid**
There are no more seats available for Madrid

**I'd like to reserve a seat**
Quería reservar un asiento
*keh-ree-a reh-sair-var oon ass-yentoh*

**Is this the right train/bus for Almeria?**
¿Es éste el tren/autobús para Almería?
*ess esteh el tren/owtoh-booss parra almeh-ree-a*

**Is this the right platform for the Seville train?**
¿Es éste el andén para el tren de Sevilla?
*ess esteh el an-den parra el tren deh sev-ee-ya*

**Which platform for the Granada train?**
¿Cuál es el andén para el tren de Granada?
*kwahl ess el an-den parra el tren deh granahda*

**Is the train/bus late?**
¿Lleva retraso el tren/autobús?
*yeh-va reh-trah-soh el tren/owtoh-booss*

**Could you help me with my luggage, please?**
¿Puede ayudarme con estas maletas, por favor?
*pweh-deh ayoodar-meh kon estass maleh-tas por fa-vor*

**Is this a nonsmoking car?**
¿Está prohibido fumar aquí?
*esta pro-ee-beedoh foomar akee*

**Is this seat free?**
¿Está libre este asiento?
*esta leebreh esteh ass-yentoh*

**This seat is taken**
Este asiento está ocupado
*esteh ass-yentoh esta okoopah-doh*

**I have reserved this seat**
Tengo reservado este asiento
*teng-goh reh-sair-vah-doh esteh ass-yentoh*

**May I open/close the window?**
¿Puedo abrir/cerrar la ventana?
*pweh-doh abreer/therrar la ventah-nu*

**When do we arrive in Bilbao?**
¿A qué hora llegamos a Bilbao?
*a keh ora yeh-gah-moss a beelbah-oh*

**What station is this?**
¿Qué estación es ésta?
*keh estath-yon ess esta*

**Do we stop at Aranjuez?**
¿Paramos en Aranjuez?
*parah-moss en aran-Hweth*

**Is there a dining car on this train?**
¿Lleva vagón-restaurante este tren?
*yeh-va va-gon restow-ranteh esteh tren*

**Where is the nearest subway station?**
¿Dónde está la estación de metro más cercana?
*dondeh esta la estath-yon deh meh-troh mass thair-kah-na*

**Where is there a bus stop?**
¿Dónde hay una parada de autobús?
*dondeh I oona parah-da deh owtoh-booss*

**Which buses go to Merida?**
¿Qué autobuses van a Mérida?
*keh owtoh-boossess van a meh-reeda*

**How often do the buses to Madrid run?**
¿Cada cuánto tiempo pasan los autobuses para Madrid?
*kah-da kwantoh tyempoh pah-san loss owtoh-boossess parra madree*

**Will you let me know when we're there?**
¿Puede avisarme cuando lleguemos?
*pweh-deh aveess-armeh kwandoh yeh-geh-moss*

**Do I have to get off yet?**
¿Tengo que bajarme ya?
*teng-goh keh ba-Harmeh ya*

**How do you get to Nerja?**
¿Cómo se va a Nerja?
*koh-moh seh va a nair-Ha*

**Do you go near San Pedro?**
¿Pasa usted cerca de San Pedro?
*pah-sa oosteh thair-ka deh san peh-droh*

## TAXI AND BOAT

**Where can I get a taxi?**
¿Dónde puedo tomar un taxi?
*dondeh pweh-doh tomar oon taksee*

**I want to go to …**
Quiero ir a …
*kee-eh-roh eer a*

**Can you let me off here?**
Pare aquí, por favor
*pah-reh akee por fa-vor*

**How much is it to El Escorial?**
¿Cuánto cuesta ir a El Escorial?
*kwantoh kwesta eer a el eskoree-al*

**Could you wait here for me and take me back?**
¿Puede esperarme aquí y llevarme de vuelta?
*pweh-deh espeh-rar-meh akee ee yeh-var-meh deh vwelta*

**Where can I get a ferry to Palma?**
¿Dónde se puede coger un ferry para Palma?
*dondeh seh pweh-deh koh-Hair oon ferree parra palma*

## THINGS YOU'LL SEE

| | |
|---|---|
| abstenerse de fumar | no smoking, please |
| aduana | customs |
| adultos | adults |
| a los andenes | to the trains |
| andén | platform |
| asientos | seats |
| automotor | local short-distance train |
| AVE | high-speed train |
| billete/billetes | ticket/tickets, ticket office |
| billete de andén | platform ticket |
| bocadillos | sandwiches, snacks |
| bonobús | book of 10 bus tickets |
| cambio de moneda | currency exchange |
| coche-cama | sleeping car |
| consigna | luggage storage office |
| control de pasaportes | passport control |
| demora | delay |
| días azules | cheap travel days |
| domingos y festivos | Sundays and national holidays |
| entrada | entrance |
| entrada por delante/por detrás | entry at the front/rear |
| equipaje | luggage |
| escala | intermediate stop |
| estación principal | central station |
| excepto domingos | Sundays excepted |
| exprés | slow night train |
| facturación | check-in |
| ferrobús | local short-distance train |
| fumadores | smokers |
| hacer transbordo en … | change at … |
| hora local | local time |
| horario | timetable |
| laborables | weekdays |

→

| | |
|---|---|
| libre | vacant |
| llegadas | arrivals |
| multa por uso indebido | penalty for misuse |
| nacional | domestic |
| niños | children |
| no fumadores | nonsmokers |
| no para en … | does not stop in … |
| ocupado | occupied |
| pague el importe exacto | no change given |
| parada | stop |
| prensa | newsstand |
| prohibida la entrada | no entry |
| prohibido asomarse a la ventana | do not lean out of the window |
| prohibido el paso | no entry |
| prohibido fumar | no smoking |
| prohibido hablar con el conductor | do not speak to the driver |
| puerto | harbor |
| puerta de embarque | gate |
| puesto de periódicos | newsstand |
| rápido | slow train stopping at all stations |
| recogida de equipajes | baggage claim |
| RENFE | Spanish national railroads |
| reserva de asientos | seat reservation |
| retraso | delay |
| ruta | route |
| sala de espera | waiting room |
| salida | departure; exit |
| salida de emergencia | emergency exit |
| salidas | departures |
| sólo laborables | weekdays only |
| suplemento | supplement |
| TAF | slow diesel train |
| TALGO | fast diesel train |

→

| | |
|---|---|
| **taquilla** | ticket office |
| **tarjeta** | travel card |
| **TER** | fast diesel train |
| **terminal** | terminal |
| **trenes de cercanías** | local trains |
| **utilice solo moneda fraccionaria** | small change only |
| **vagón** | passenger car |
| **viaje** | trip |
| **vuelo** | flight |
| **vuelo directo** | direct flight |
| **vuelo regular** | scheduled flight |

## Things You'll Hear

**¿Tiene equipaje?**
Do you have any luggage?

**¿Fumadores o no fumadores?**
Smoking or nonsmoking?

**¿Asiento de ventanilla o de pasillo?**
Window seat or aisle seat?

**Su billete, por favor**
Can I see your ticket, please?

**Los pasajeros del vuelo dos dos uno, con destino a Chicago, están en estos momentos embarcando**
Passengers for flight 221 for Chicago are requested to board

**Diríjanse a la puerta (número) cuatro**
Please go to gate (number) four now

→

**Completo**
It's full

**Los billetes, por favor**
Tickets, please

**Suban al tren**
Board the train

**El tren con destino a Granada va a efectuar su salida del andén número seis dentro de diez minutos**
The train for Granada will leave from platform six in ten minutes

**El tren procedente de Madrid va a efectuar su llegada al andén número uno dentro de cinco minutos**
The train from Madrid will arrive at platform one in five minutes

**El tren con destino a Sevilla lleva quince minutos de retraso**
The train for Seville is running 15 minutes late

**Saquen sus billetes, por favor**
Have your tickets ready, please

**Su pasaporte, por favor**
Your passport, please

**Abra sus maletas, por favor**
Open your suitcases, please

# EATING OUT

You can eat in a variety of places:

**Restaurante:** These have an official rating (1–5 forks), but this depends more on the variety of dishes served than on the quality.

**Cafetería:** Not to be confused with the American term. It is a combined bar, café, and restaurant. Service is provided at the counter or, for a little extra, at a table. There is usually a good variety of fixed-price menus at reasonable prices (look for **platos combinados**).

**Fonda:** Offers inexpensive, good food that is representative of regional dishes.

**Hostería or Hostal:** A restaurant that usually specializes in regional dishes.

**Parador:** Belonging to the previously state-run hotels, they offer a first-rate service in select surroundings.

**Café or Bar:** Both are general cafés selling all kinds of food and drink (again, they are not to be confused with American establishments of the same name). Well worth trying if you just want a quick snack. In some places, they serve free **tapas** (appetizers) with alcoholic drinks. Full meals are often available.

**Merendero:** Outdoor **café** on the coast or in the country. Usually inexpensive and a good buy.

Breakfast in Spain is at 8 AM, lunch is at 2 PM, and dinner (the main evening meal) is at 10 PM.

## USEFUL WORDS AND PHRASES

| appetizer | el primer plato | *primair plah-toh* |
|---|---|---|
| beer | una cerveza | *thairveh-tha* |
| bottle | la botella | *boh-tay-ya* |

| bread | el pan | *pan* |
|---|---|---|
| butter | la mantequilla | *manteh-kee-ya* |
| café | una cafetería | *kaffeh-teh-ree-a* |
| cake | un pastel | *pastell* |
| carafe | una jarra | *Harra* |
| check | la cuenta | *kwenta* |
| chef | el cocinero | *kothee-neh-roh* |
| children's | una ración especial | *rath-yon espethyal* |
| portion | para niños | *parra neen-yoss* |
| coffee | el café | *kaffeh* |
| cup | la taza | *tah-tha* |
| dessert | el postre | *postreh* |
| fork | el tenedor | *teneh-dor* |
| glass | el vaso | *vah-soh* |
| half liter | medio litro | *meh-dyoh leetroh* |
| knife | el cuchillo | *kootchee-yoh* |
| liter | litro | *leetroh* |
| main course | el segundo plato | *segoondoh plah-toh* |
| menu | la carta | *karta* |
| milk | la leche | *letcheh* |
| napkin | la servilleta | *sairvee-yeh-ta* |
| pepper | la pimienta | *peemyenta* |
| plate | el plato | *plah-toh* |
| receipt | un recibo | *retheeboh* |
| restaurant | un restaurante | *restowranteh* |
| salt | la sal | *sal* |
| sandwich | un sandwich | *sand-weetch* |
| (*Spanish*) | un bocadillo | *boh-kadee-yoh* |
| soup | la sopa | *soh-pa* |
| spoon | la cuchara | *kootchah-ra* |
| sugar | el azúcar | *athookar* |
| table | una mesa | *meh-sa* |
| tea | el té | *teh* |
| teaspoon | la cucharilla | *kootcha-ree-ya* |
| tip | una propina | *propeena* |
| waiter | el camarero | *kamma-reh-roh* |

| **waitress** | la camarera | *kamma-reh-ra* |
| **water** | el agua | *ahg-wa* |
| **wine** | el vino | *veenoh* |
| **wine list** | la carta de vinos | *karta deh veenoss* |

### A table for one, please
Una mesa para una persona, por favor
*oona meh-sa parra oona pairsoh-na por fa-vor*

### A table for two/three, please
Una mesa para dos/tres personas, por favor
*oona meh-sa parra doss/tress pairsoh-nass por fa-vor*

### Is there a highchair?
¿Hay sillita de niño?
*i see-yeeta deh neen-yo*

### Can we see the menu/wine list?
¿Nos trae la carta/la carta de vinos?
*noss trah-eh la karta/la karta deh veenoss*

### What would you recommend?
¿Qué recomendaría usted?
*keh rekomenda-ree-a oosteh*

### I'd like …
Quería …
*keh-ree-a*

### Just a cup of coffee, please
Un café nada más, por favor
*oon kaffeh nah-da mass por fa-vor*

### I only want a snack
Sólo quiero una comida ligera
*soh-loh kee-eh-roh oona kommeeda lee-Heh-ra*

### Is there a fixed-price menu?
¿Hay menú del día?
*i meh-noo dell dee-a*

**A liter carafe of house red, please**
Una jarra de litro de tinto de la casa, por favor
*oona Harra deh leetroh deh teentoh deh la kah-sa por fa-vor*

**Do you have any vegetarian dishes?**
¿Tiene algún plato vegetariano?
*tyeh-neh algoon plah-toh veh-Hetaryah-noh*

**I'm allergic to nuts/shellfish**
Soy alérgico a los frutos secos/marisco
*soy allairheekoh a los frootos sekos/mareesko*

**Could we have some water?**
¿Nos trae agua, por favor?
*noss trah-eh ahg-wa por fa-vor*

**Two more beers, please**
Dos cervezas más, por favor
*doss thair-veh-thass mass por fa-vor*

**Do you have children's portions?**
¿Tiene raciones especiales para niños?
*tyeh-neh rathyoh-ness espethyah-less parra neen-yoss*

**Can you warm this bottle/baby food for me?**
¿Podría calentar este biberón/comida para niño?
*po-dreea kalentar este beeberon/komeeda parra neen-yoh*

**Waiter/waitress!**
¡Oiga, por favor!
*oy-gah por fa-vor*

**I didn't order this**
No he pedido esto
*noh eh pedeedoh estoh*

**You've forgotten to bring my dessert**
Se ha olvidado de traerme el postre
*seh a olveedah-doh deh trah-airmeh el postreh*

**May we have some more …?**
¿Nos trae más …?
noss *trah-eh* mass

**Can I have another knife/fork?**
¿Me trae otro cuchillo/tenedor?
meh *trah-eh otroh kootchee-yoh/teneh-dor*

**May we have the check, please?**
¿Nos trae la cuenta, por favor?
noss *trah-eh la kwenta por fa-vor*

**Could I have a receipt, please?**
¿Me puede dar un recibo, por favor?
meh *pweh-deh dar oon retheeboh por fa-vor*

**Can we pay separately?**
Queríamos pagar por separado
*keh-ree-amoss pagar por separah-doh*

**The meal was very good, thank you**
La comida ha sido muy buena, gracias
*la kommeeda a seedoh mwee bweh-na grath-yass*

---

### THINGS YOU'LL HEAR

**¡Que (le/les) aproveche!**
Enjoy your meal!

**¿Qué quiere beber/tomar?**
What would you like to drink?

**¿Le ha gustado la comida?**
Did you enjoy your meal?

---

# MENU GUIDE

| | |
|---|---|
| aceitunas | olives |
| acelgas | spinach beet |
| achicoria | chicory |
| aguacate | avocado |
| ahumados | smoked fish |
| ajo | garlic |
| albaricoques | apricots |
| albóndigas | meatballs |
| alcachofas | artichokes |
| alcachofas con jamón | artichokes with ham |
| alcachofas salteadas | sautéed artichokes |
| alcachofas a la vinagreta | artichokes vinaigrette |
| alcaparras | capers |
| almejas | clams |
| almejas a la marinera | clams stewed in wine and parsley |
| almejas naturales | live clams |
| almendras | almonds |
| alubias con ... | beans with ... |
| ancas de rana | frogs' legs |
| anchoas | anchovies |
| anguila | eel |
| angulas | baby eels |
| anís | aniseed-flavored alcoholic drink |
| arenque | herring |
| arroz a la cubana | rice with fried eggs and banana fritters |
| arroz a la valenciana | rice with seafood |
| arroz con leche | rice pudding |
| asados | roast meats |
| atún | tuna |
| avellanas | hazelnuts |
| azúcar | sugar |
| bacalao a la vizcaína | cod served with ham, peppers, and chilis |
| bacalao al pil pil | cod served with chilis and garlic |
| batido de chocolate | chocolate milk shake |
| batido de fresa | strawberry milk shake |
| batido de frutas | fruit milk shake |
| batido de vainilla | vanilla milk shake |
| bebidas | drinks |

| | |
|---|---|
| berenjenas | eggplant |
| besugo al horno | baked sea bream |
| bistec de ternera | veal steak |
| bizcochos | ladyfingers |
| bonito al horno | baked tunafish |
| bonito con tomate | tuna with tomato |
| boquerones fritos | fried anchovies |
| brazo gitano | swiss roll |
| brevas | figs |
| brocheta de riñones | kidney kebabs |
| buñuelos | light fried pastries |
| butifarra | Catalan sausage (made with a large proportion of bacon) |
| cabrito asado | roast goat |
| cachelada | pork stew with eggs, tomato, and onion |
| café | coffee |
| café con leche | coffee with steamed milk |
| calabacines | zucchini, vegetable marrow |
| calabaza | pumpkin |
| calamares a la romana | squid rings in batter |
| calamares en su tinta | squid cooked in their ink |
| calamares fritos | fried squid |
| caldeirada | fish soup |
| caldereta gallega | vegetable stew |
| caldo de ... | ... soup |
| caldo de gallina | chicken soup |
| caldo de pescado | clear fish soup |
| caldo gallego | vegetable soup |
| caldo guanche | soup made with potatoes, onions, tomatoes, and zucchini |
| callos a la madrileña | tripe cooked with chilis |
| camarones | baby prawns |
| canelones | cannelloni |
| cangrejos de río | river crabs |
| caracoles | snails |
| caramelos | candies |
| carnes | meats |
| carro de queso | cheese board |
| castañas | chestnuts |
| cebolla | onion |
| cebolletas | spring onions |

| | |
|---|---|
| centollo | spider crab |
| cerezas | cherries |
| cerveza | beer |
| cesta de frutas | a selection of fresh fruit |
| champiñón a la crema | mushrooms in cream sauce |
| champiñón al ajillo | mushrooms with garlic |
| champiñón a la plancha | grilled mushrooms |
| champiñón salteado | sautéed mushrooms |
| chanquetes | fish (similar to whitebait) |
| chateaubrian | Chateaubriand steak (thick steak) |
| chipirones | baby squid |
| chipirones en su tinta | squid cooked in their ink |
| chipirones rellenos | stuffed squid |
| chirimoyas | custard apples |
| chocos | squid |
| chuleta de buey | beef chop |
| chuleta de cerdo | pork chop |
| chuleta de cerdo empanada | breaded pork chop |
| chuleta de cordero | lamb chop |
| chuleta de ternera | veal chop |
| chuleta de ternera empanada | breaded veal chop |
| chuletas de cordero empanadas | breaded lamb chops |
| chuletas de lomo ahumado | smoked pork chops |
| chuletitas de cordero | small lamb chops |
| chuletón | large chop |
| chuletón de buey | large beef chop |
| churros | deep-fried pastry strips |
| cigalas | crayfish |
| cigalas cocidas | boiled crayfish |
| ciruelas | plums, greengages |
| ciruelas pasas | prunes |
| cochinillo asado | roast suckling pig |
| cocido | stew made with meat, chickpeas, and vegetables |
| cocktail de bogavante | lobster cocktail |
| cocochas (de merluza) | hake stew |
| cóctel de gambas | shrimp cocktail |
| cóctel de langostinos | jumbo shrimp cocktail |
| cóctel de mariscos | seafood cocktail |
| codornices | quail |
| codornices asadas | roast quail |

| | |
|---|---|
| codornices con uvas | quail stewed with grapes |
| codornices escabechadas | marinated quail |
| codornices estofadas | braised quail |
| col | cabbage |
| coles de Bruselas | Brussels sprouts |
| coles de Bruselas salteadas | sautéed Brussels sprouts |
| coliflor | cauliflower |
| coliflor con bechamel | cauliflower with white sauce |
| coñac | brandy |
| conejo asado | roast rabbit |
| conejo encebollado | rabbit served with onions |
| conejo estofado | braised rabbit |
| congrio | conger eel |
| consomé al jerez | consommé with sherry |
| consomé con yema | consommé with egg yolk |
| consomé de ave | fowl consommé |
| consomé de pollo | chicken consommé |
| contra de ternera con guisantes | veal stew with peas |
| contrafilete de ternera | veal fillet |
| copa … | … cup, glass of wine |
| copa de helado | ice cream, assorted flavors |
| cordero asado | roast lamb |
| cordero chilindrón | lamb stew with onion, tomato, peppers, and eggs |
| costillas de cerdo | pork ribs |
| crema catalana | crème brûlée |
| cremada | dessert made with egg, sugar, and milk |
| crema de cangrejos | cream of crab soup |
| crema de espárragos | cream of asparagus soup |
| crema de legumbres | cream of vegetable soup |
| crepe imperiale | crêpe suzette |
| criadillas de tierra | truffles, usually served with meat dishes |
| crocante | ice cream with chopped nuts |
| croquetas | croquettes |
| croquetas de jamón | ham croquettes |
| croquetas de pescado | fish croquettes |
| cuajada | curds |
| dátiles | dates |
| embutidos | sausages |
| embutidos de la tierra | local sausages |
| embutidos variados | assorted sausages |

| | |
|---|---|
| empanada gallega | fish pie |
| empanada santiaguesa | fish pie |
| empanadillas de bonito | small tuna pies |
| empanadillas de carne | small meat pies |
| empanadillas de chorizo | Spanish sausage pies |
| endivias | endive |
| ensaimada mallorquina | large, spiral-shaped bun |
| ensalada de arenque | fish salad |
| ensalada de atún | tuna salad |
| ensalada de frutas | fruit salad |
| ensalada de gambas | shrimp salad |
| ensalada de lechuga | lettuce salad |
| ensalada de pollo | chicken salad |
| ensalada de tomate | tomato salad |
| ensalada ilustrada | mixed salad |
| ensalada mixta | mixed salad |
| ensalada simple | green salad |
| ensalada | Spanish salad |
| ensaladilla rusa | Russian salad (potatoes, carrots, peas, and other vegetables in mayonnaise) |
| entrecot a la parrilla | grilled entrecôte |
| entrecot de ternera | veal entrecôte |
| entremeses de la casa | hors d'oeuvres, appetizers |
| entremeses variados | hors d'oeuvres, appetizers |
| escalope a la milanesa | breaded veal with cheese |
| escalope a la parrilla | grilled veal |
| escalope a la plancha | grilled veal |
| escalope de lomo de cerdo | escalope of pork fillet |
| escalope de ternera | veal scallop |
| escalope empanado | breaded scallops |
| escalopines al vino de Marsala | veal scallops cooked in wine |
| escalopines de ternera | veal scallops |
| escarola | escarole |
| espadín a la toledana | kabob |
| espaguetis italiana | spaghetti |
| espárragos | asparagus |
| espárragos con mayonesa | asparagus with mayonnaise |
| espárragos trigueros | green asparagus |
| espinacas | spinach |
| espinacas a la crema | creamed spinach |
| espinazo de cerdo con patatas | stew of pork ribs with potatoes |

| | |
|---|---|
| estofado de … | … stew |
| estofado de liebre | hare stew |
| estofados | stews |
| estragón | tarragon |
| fabada (asturiana) | bean stew with sausage |
| faisán con castañas | pheasant with chestnuts |
| faisán estofado | stewed pheasant |
| faisán trufado | pheasant with truffles |
| fiambres | cold meats |
| fideos | thin pasta, noodles |
| filete a la parrilla | grilled beef |
| filete de cerdo | pork steak |
| filete de ternera | veal steak |
| flan | crème caramel |
| flan al ron | crème caramel with rum |
| flan de caramelo | crème caramel |
| fresas con nata | strawberries and cream |
| fruta | fruit |
| frutas en almíbar | fruit in syrup |
| fruta variada | assorted fresh fruit |
| gallina en pepitoria | chicken stewed with peppers |
| gambas al ajillo | garlic shrimp |
| gambas a la americana | shrimp |
| gambas a la plancha | grilled shrimp |
| gambas cocidas | boiled shrimp |
| gambas con mayonesa | shrimp with mayonnaise |
| gambas en gabardina | shrimp in batter |
| gambas rebozadas | shrimp in batter |
| garbanzos | chickpeas |
| garbanzos a la catalana | chickpeas with sausage, boiled eggs, and pine nuts |
| gazpacho andaluz | cold tomato soup from Andalusia |
| gelatina de … | … gelatin |
| gratén de … | … au gratin (baked in a cream and cheese sauce) |
| grelo | turnip |
| guisantes con jamón | peas with ham |
| guisantes salteados | sautéed peas |
| habas | broad beans |
| habas con jamón | broad beans with ham |
| habas fritas | fried young broad beans |

| | |
|---|---|
| habichuelas | beans |
| helado de caramelo | caramel ice cream |
| helado de chocolate | chocolate ice cream |
| helado de fresa | strawberry ice cream |
| helado de mantecado | vanilla ice cream |
| helado de turrón | nut ice cream |
| helado de vainilla | vanilla ice cream |
| hígado | liver |
| hígado con cebolla | liver cooked with onion |
| hígado de ternera estofado | braised calf's liver |
| hígado estofado | braised liver |
| higos con miel y nueces | figs with honey and nuts |
| higos secos | dried figs |
| horchata (de chufas) | cold almond-flavored milk drink |
| huevo hilado | egg yolk garnish |
| huevos | eggs |
| huevos a la flamenca | fried eggs with ham, tomato, and vegetables |
| huevos cocidos | hard-boiled eggs |
| huevos con jamón | eggs with ham |
| huevos duros | hard-boiled eggs |
| huevos duros con mayonesa | boiled eggs with mayonnaise |
| huevos con panceta | eggs and bacon |
| huevos con patatas fritas | fried eggs and french fries |
| huevos con picadillo | eggs with minced sausage |
| huevos con salchichas | eggs and sausages |
| huevos escalfados | poached eggs |
| huevos fritos | fried eggs |
| huevos fritos con chorizo | fried eggs with Spanish sausage |
| huevos fritos con jamón | fried eggs with ham |
| huevos pasados por agua | soft-boiled eggs |
| huevos rellenos | stuffed eggs |
| huevos revueltos con tomate | scrambled eggs with tomato |
| jamón con huevo hilado | ham with egg yolk garnish |
| jamón de Jabugo | Spanish ham |
| jamón de Trevélez | Spanish ham |
| jamón serrano | cured ham |
| jarra de vino | wine jug |
| jerez amontillado | pale dry sherry |
| jerez fino | pale light sherry |
| jerez oloroso | sweet sherry |
| jeta | pigs' cheeks |

| | |
|---|---|
| judías verdes | green beans |
| judías verdes a la española | bean stew |
| judías verdes al natural | plain green beans |
| judías verdes con jamón | green beans with ham |
| jugo de albaricoque | apricot juice |
| jugo de lima | lime juice |
| jugo de limón | lemon juice |
| jugo de melocotón | peach juice |
| jugo de naranja | orange juice |
| jugo de piña | pineapple juice |
| jugo de tomate | tomato juice |
| Jumilla | light red and white "mistela" wines |
| langosta a la americana | lobster with brandy and garlic |
| langosta a la catalana | lobster with mushrooms and ham in a white sauce |
| langosta fría con mayonesa | cold lobster with mayonnaise |
| langosta gratinada | lobster au gratin |
| langostinos a la plancha | grilled jumbo shrimp |
| langostinos con mayonesa | jumbo shrimp with mayonnaise |
| langostinos dos salsas | jumbo shrimp cooked in two sauces |
| laurel | bay leaves |
| leche frita | pudding made from milk and eggs |
| leche merengada | cold milk with meringues |
| lechuga | lettuce |
| lengua de buey | ox tongue |
| lengua de cordero estofada | stewed lambs' tongue |
| lenguado a la parrilla | grilled sole |
| lenguado a la plancha | grilled sole |
| lenguado a la romana | sole in batter |
| lenguado frito | fried sole |
| lenguado grillado | grilled sole |
| lenguado meuniere | sole meunière (sole dipped in flour, fried, and served with butter, lemon juice, and parsley) |
| lentejas | lentils |
| lentejas aliñadas | lentils in vinaigrette dressing |
| licores | spirits, liqueurs |
| liebre estofada | stewed hare |
| lombarda rellena | stuffed red cabbage |
| lombarda salteada | sautéed red cabbage |
| lomo curado | pork loin sausage |

| | |
|---|---|
| lonchas de jamón | sliced, cured ham |
| longaniza | cooked Spanish sausage |
| lubina a la marinera | sea bass in a parsley sauce |
| lubina al horno | baked sea bass |
| macarrones | macaroni |
| macarrones gratinados | macaroni and cheese |
| macedonia de fruta | fruit salad |
| Málaga | sweet wine |
| mandarinas | tangerines |
| manises | peanuts |
| manitas de cordero | lamb shank |
| manos de cerdo | pigs' feet |
| manos de cerdo a la parrilla | grilled pigs' feet |
| mantecadas | small sponge cakes |
| mantequilla | butter |
| manzanas | apples |
| manzanas asadas | baked apples |
| manzanilla | dry sherry-type wine |
| mariscada | cold mixed shellfish |
| mariscos del día | fresh shellfish |
| mariscos del tiempo | seasonal shellfish |
| mazapán | marzipan |
| medallones de anguila | eel steaks |
| medallones de merluza | hake steaks |
| media de agua | half bottle of mineral water |
| mejillones | mussels |
| mejillones a la marinera | mussels in a wine sauce |
| melocotón | peach |
| melocotones en almíbar | peaches in syrup |
| melón | melon |
| melón con jamón | melon with ham |
| membrillo | quince jelly |
| menestra de legumbres | vegetable stew |
| menú de la casa | fixed-price menu |
| menú del día | fixed-price menu |
| merluza a la cazuela | stewed hake |
| merluza a la parrilla | grilled hake |
| merluza a la plancha | grilled hake |
| merluza a la riojana | hake with chilis |
| merluza a la romana | hake steaks in batter |
| merluza a la vasca | hake in a garlic sauce |

| | |
|---|---|
| merluza al ajo arriero | hake with garlic and chillis |
| merluza en salsa | hake in sauce |
| merluza en salsa verde | hake in a parsley and wine sauce |
| merluza fría | cold hake |
| merluza frita | fried hake |
| mermelada | jam |
| mermelada de albaricoque | apricot jam |
| mermelada de ciruelas | prune jam |
| mermelada de frambuesas | raspberry jam |
| mermelada de fresas | strawberry jam |
| mermelada de limón | lemon marmalade |
| mermelada de melocotón | peach jam |
| mermelada de naranja | orange marmalade |
| mero | grouper (type of fish) |
| mero a la parrilla | grilled grouper |
| mero en salsa verde | grouper in garlic and parsley sauce |
| mollejas de ternera fritas | fried sweetbreads |
| morcilla | blood sausage |
| morcilla de carnero | blood sausage made from mutton |
| morros de cerdo | pigs' cheeks |
| morros de vaca | cows' cheeks |
| mortadela | salami-type sausage |
| morteruelo | kind of pâté |
| mousse de chocolate | chocolate mousse |
| mousse de limón | lemon mousse |
| nabo | turnip |
| naranjas | oranges |
| natillas | cold custard |
| natillas de chocolate | cold custard with chocolate |
| níscalos | wild mushrooms |
| nísperos | medlars (fruit similar to crab apple) |
| nueces | walnuts |
| orejas de cerdo | pigs' ears |
| otros mariscos según precios en plaza | other shellfish, depending on current prices |
| paella | fried rice with various seafood and chicken |
| paella castellana | meat paella |
| paella de marisco | shellfish paella |
| paella de pollo | chicken paella |
| paella valenciana | shellfish, rabbit, and chicken paella |
| paleta de cordero lechal | shoulder of lamb |

| | |
|---|---|
| pan | bread |
| pan de higos | dried fig cake with cinnamon |
| panache de verduras | vegetable stew |
| panceta | bacon |
| parrillada de caza | mixed grilled game |
| parrillada de mariscos | mixed grilled shellfish |
| pasas | raisins |
| pastel de ... | ... cake |
| pastel de ternera | veal pie |
| pasteles | cakes |
| patatas a la pescadora | potatoes with fish |
| patatas asadas | baked potatoes |
| patatas bravas | potatoes in cayenne pepper sauce |
| patatas fritas | french fries |
| patitos rellenos | stuffed duckling |
| pato a la naranja | duck à l'orange |
| pato asado | roast duck |
| pato estofado | stewed duck |
| pavo asado | roast turkey |
| pavo relleno | stuffed turkey |
| pavo trufado | turkey stuffed with truffles |
| pecho de ternera | breast of veal |
| pechuga de pollo | breast of chicken |
| pepinillos | pickles |
| pepinillos en vinagreta | pickles in vinaigrette sauce |
| pepino | cucumber |
| peras | pears |
| percebes | edible barnacle (shellfish) |
| perdices a la campesina | partridges with vegetables |
| perdices a la manchega | partridges in red wine with garlic, herbs, and pepper |
| perdices asadas | roast partridges |
| perdices con chocolate | partridges with chocolate sauce |
| perdices escabechadas | marinated partridges |
| perejil | parsley |
| pescaditos fritos | fried fish |
| pestiños | sugared pastries flavored with aniseed |
| pez espada ahumado | smoked swordfish |
| picadillo de ternera | minced veal |
| pimienta | black pepper |
| pimientos a la riojana | baked red peppers fried in oil and garlic |

| | |
|---|---|
| pimientos fritos | fried peppers |
| pimientos morrones | bell peppers |
| pimientos rellenos | stuffed peppers |
| pimientos verdes | green peppers |
| piña al gratín | pineapple au gratin |
| piña fresca | fresh pineapple |
| pinchitos | snacks served in bars |
| pinchos | snacks served in bars |
| pinchos morunos | kebabs |
| piñones | pine nuts |
| pisto | fried mixed vegetables |
| pisto manchego | vegetable marrow with onion and tomato |
| plátanos | bananas |
| plátanos flameados | flambéed bananas |
| pollo a la parrilla | grilled chicken |
| pollo a la riojana | chicken with peppers and chilis |
| pollo al ajillo | fried chicken with garlic |
| pollo al champaña | chicken in champagne |
| pollo al vino blanco | chicken in white wine |
| pollo asado | roast chicken |
| pollo braseado | braised chicken |
| pollo con tomate | chicken with tomatoes |
| pollo con verduras | chicken and vegetables |
| pollo en cacerola | chicken casserole |
| pollo en pepitoria | chicken in wine with saffron, garlic, and almonds |
| pollo salteado | sautéed chicken |
| pollos tomateros con zanahorias | young chicken with carrots |
| polvorones | sugar-based dessert eaten at Christmas |
| pomelo | grapefruit |
| potaje castellano | thick broth |
| potaje de garbanzos | chickpea stew |
| potaje de habichuelas | white bean stew |
| potaje de lentejas | lentil stew |
| puchero canario | casserole of meat, chickpeas, and corn |
| pulpitos con cebolla | baby octopus with onions |
| pulpo | octopus |
| puré de patatas | mashed potatoes, potato purée |
| purrusalda | cod with leeks and potatoes |
| queso con membrillo | cheese with quince jelly |
| queso de Burgos | soft white cheese |

| | |
|---|---|
| queso de bola | Dutch cheese |
| queso de oveja | sheep's cheese |
| queso del país | local cheese |
| queso gallego | creamy cheese |
| queso manchego | hard, strong cheese |
| quisquillas | shrimps |
| rábanos | radish |
| ragout de ternera | veal ragoût |
| rape a la americana | monkfish with brandy and herbs |
| rape a la cazuela | stewed monkfish |
| rape a la plancha | grilled monkfish |
| raviolis | ravioli |
| raya | skate |
| redondo al horno | roast fillet of beef |
| remolacha | beets |
| repollo | cabbage |
| repostería de la casa | cakes baked on the premises |
| requesón | cream cheese, cottage cheese |
| revuelto de ajos tiernos | scrambled eggs with spring garlic |
| revuelto de angulas | scrambled eggs with baby eels |
| revuelto de gambas | scrambled eggs with shrimps |
| revuelto de sesos | scrambled eggs with brains |
| revuelto de trigueros | scrambled eggs with asparagus |
| revuelto mixto | scrambled eggs with mixed vegetables |
| Ribeiro | type of white wine |
| riñones | kidneys |
| riñones al jerez | kidneys with sherry |
| Rioja | red or white wine—considered the finest wine in Spain |
| rodaballo | turbot (fish) |
| romero | rosemary |
| ron | rum |
| roscas | sweet pastries |
| sal | salt |
| salchichas | sausages |
| salchichas de Frankfurt | hot dogs |
| salchichón | white sausage with pepper |
| salmón a la parrilla | grilled salmon |
| salmón ahumado | smoked salmon |
| salmón frío | cold salmon |
| salmonetes | red mullet |

| | |
|---|---|
| salmonetes a la parrilla | grilled red mullet |
| salmonetes en papillote | red mullet cooked in foil |
| salmorejo | thick sauce made with bread, tomatoes, olive oil, vinegar, green pepper, and garlic, usually served with hard-boiled eggs |
| salpicón de mariscos | shellfish vinaigrette |
| salsa allioli or ali oli | mayonnaise with garlic |
| salsa bechamel | white sauce |
| salsa de tomate | tomato sauce |
| salsa holandesa | hollandaise sauce (hot sauce made with eggs and butter) |
| salsa mahonesa or mayonesa | mayonnaise |
| salsa tártara | tartare sauce |
| salsa vinagreta | vinaigrette sauce |
| sandía | watermelon |
| sangría | sangría (mixture of red wine, lemonade, liquor, and fruit) |
| sardinas a la brasa | barbecued sardines |
| sardinas a la parrilla | grilled sardines |
| sardinas fritas | fried sardines |
| seco | dry |
| semidulce | medium-sweet |
| sesos a la romana | fried brains in batter |
| sesos rebozados | brains in batter |
| setas a la plancha | grilled mushrooms |
| setas rellenas | stuffed mushrooms |
| sidra | cider |
| sobreasada | soft red sausage with cayenne pepper |
| solomillo con guisantes | fillet steak with peas |
| solomillo con patatas | fillet steak with french fries |
| solomillo de ternera | fillet of veal |
| solomillo de vaca | fillet of beef |
| solomillo frío | cold roast beef |
| sopa | soup |
| sopa castellana | vegetable soup |
| sopa de ajo | garlic soup |
| sopa de almendras | almond-based pudding |
| sopa de cola de buey | oxtail soup |
| sopa de fideos | noodle soup |
| sopa de gallina | chicken soup |

| | |
|---|---|
| sopa del día | soup of the day |
| sopa de legumbres | vegetable soup |
| sopa de lentejas | lentil soup |
| sopa de marisco | fish and shellfish soup |
| sopa de pescado | fish soup |
| sopa de rabo de buey | oxtail soup |
| sopa de verduras | vegetable soup |
| sopa mallorquina | soup with tomato, meat, and eggs |
| sopa sevillana | fish and mayonnaise soup |
| sorbete | sorbet |
| soufflé | soufflé |
| soufflé de fresones | strawberry soufflé |
| soufflé de naranja | orange soufflé |
| soufflé de queso | cheese soufflé |
| suplemento de verduras | extra vegetables |
| tallarines | noodles |
| tallarines a la italiana | tagliatelle |
| tarta de almendra | almond cake |
| tarta de chocolate | chocolate cake |
| tarta de fresas | strawberry tart or cake |
| tarta de la casa | cake baked on the premises |
| tarta de manzana | apple tart |
| tarta helada | ice cream cake |
| tarta moca | mocha tart |
| tencas | tench |
| ternera asada | roast veal |
| tocinillos del cielo | crème caramel |
| tomates rellenos | stuffed tomatoes |
| tomillo | thyme |
| tordo | thrush |
| torrijas | sweet pastries |
| tortilla Alaska | baked Alaska |
| tortilla a la paisana | omelette with a variety of vegetables |
| tortilla a su gusto | omelette made to the customer's wishes |
| tortilla de bonito | tuna omelette |
| tortilla de champiñones | mushroom omelette |
| tortilla de chorizo | omelette containing spiced sausage |
| tortilla de escabeche | fish omelette |
| tortilla de espárragos | asparagus omelette |
| tortilla de gambas | shrimp omelette |
| tortilla de jamón | ham omelette |

| | |
|---|---|
| tortilla de patatas | potato omelette |
| tortilla de sesos | brain omelette |
| tortilla de setas | mushroom omelette |
| tortilla española | Spanish omelette with potato, onion, and garlic |
| tortilla sacromonte | vegetable, brains, and sausage omelette |
| tortillas variadas | assorted omelettes |
| tournedó | tournedos (fillet steak) |
| trucha ahumada | smoked trout |
| trucha con jamón | trout with ham |
| trucha escabechada | marinated trout |
| truchas a la marinera | trout in wine sauce |
| truchas molinera | trout meunière (trout dipped in flour, fried, and served with butter, lemon juice, and parsley) |
| trufas | truffles |
| turrón | nougat |
| turrón de Alicante | hard nougat |
| turrón de Jijona | soft nougat |
| turrón de coco | coconut nougat |
| turrón de yema | nougat with egg yolk |
| uvas | grapes |
| Valdepeñas | type of fruity red wine |
| vieiras | scallops |
| vino blanco | white wine |
| vino de mesa | table wine |
| vino rosado | rosé wine |
| vino tinto | red wine |
| zanahorias a la crema | carrots à la crème |
| zarzuela de mariscos | seafood stew |
| zarzuela de pescados y mariscos | fish and shellfish stew |
| zumo de ... | ... juice |
| zumo de albaricoque | apricot juice |
| zumo de lima | lime juice |
| zumo de limón | lemon juice |
| zumo de melocotón | peach juice |
| zumo de naranja | orange juice |
| zumo de piña | pineapple juice |
| zumo de tomate | tomato juice |

# STORES AND SERVICES

This chapter covers all kinds of shopping needs and services.
To start with, you'll find some general phrases that can be used
in lots of different places—many of these are listed below.
After the general phrases come more specific requests and
sentences to use when you've found what you need, be it food,
clothing, repairs, film developing, a haircut, or bargaining in
the market. Don't forget to refer to the mini-dictionary for
items you may be looking for.

Stores can stay open as they wish, but most stick to the usual
hours of 9 AM to 1:30 PM and 4:30 PM to 7:30 PM. In summer, a
longer lunch break means that stores stay open in the evenings
from about 5 PM to 8:30 PM. Most stores close at 2 PM on
Saturdays. Large department stores do not close for lunch and
are open longer on Saturdays.

Toiletries and non-medicinal items can be bought from
supermarkets and department stores or from a **perfumería**,
where they'll probably cost a little more. (See Health, page 113,
for details about pharmacies.)

A hair salon is called a **peluquería**. A men's hair salon is often
called a **barbería**. It is easily recognized by the traditional
barber's pole or a similar device with red, white, and blue stripes.

## USEFUL WORDS AND PHRASES

| | | |
|---|---|---|
| **antiques store** | la tienda de antigüedades | *tyenda deh antee-gwehdah-dess* |
| **audio equipment** | aparatos de música | *aparah-toss deh moossika* |
| **bakery** | la panadería | *pannadeh-ree-a* |
| **bookstore** | la librería | *leebreh-ree-a* |
| **butcher's** | la carnicería | *karnee-theh-ree-a* |
| **buy** | comprar | *komprar* |
| **camera store** | la tienda de fotografía | *tyenda deh fotografee-a* |
| **camping equipment** | equipos de camping | *ekeeposs deh kampeen* |

| | | |
|---|---|---|
| **carrier bag** | una bolsa | _bolsa_ |
| **cash register** | la caja | _kah-Ha_ |
| **china** | la porcelana | _porthelah-na_ |
| **confectioner's** | la confitería | _konfeeteree-a_ |
| **cost** | costar | _kostar_ |
| **craft shop** | la tienda de artesanía | _tyenda deh artesanee-a_ |
| **department store** | los grandes almacenes | _grandess almatheh-ness_ |
| **dry cleaner's** | la tintorería | _teentoreree-a_ |
| **electrical goods store** | la tienda de electrodomésticos | _tyenda deh elektro-domestee-koss_ |
| **expensive** | caro | _kah-roh_ |
| **fish market** | la pescadería | _peskadeh-ree-a_ |
| **florist's** | la floristería | _floreess-teh-ree-a_ |
| **food store** | la tienda de alimentación | _tyenda deh aleementath-yon_ |
| **gift shop** | la tienda de regalos | _tyenda deh regah-loss_ |
| **hair salon** (_men's_) | la barbería | _barbeh-ree-a_ |
| (_women's_) | la peluquería | _pelookeh-ree-a_ |
| **hardware store** | la ferretería | _ferreh-teh-ree-a_ |
| **indoor market** | el mercado | _mairkah-doh_ |
| **inexpensive** | barato | _barah-toh_ |
| **jeweler's** | la joyería | _Hoy-ehree-a_ |
| **large department store** | el híper | _eepair_ |
| **Laundromat** | la lavandería automática | _lavanderee-a owtoh-mateeka_ |
| **liquor store** | la bodega de vinos | _boh-dehga deh veenos_ |
| **market** | el mercadillo | _mairkadee-yoh_ |
| **menswear** | caballeros | _kabayeh-ross_ |
| **newsstand** | el kiosko de periódicos | _kee-oskoh deh peh-ree-oddee-koss_ |
| **optician's** | la óptica | _opteeka_ |
| **pastry shop** | la pastelería | _pasteh-leh-ree-a_ |
| **produce market** | la frutería | _frooteree-a_ |

| | | |
|---|---|---|
| **receipt** | el recibo | *reth__ee__boh* |
| **record store** | la tienda de discos | *ty__e__nda deh d__ee__skoss* |
| **sale** | rebajas, liquidación | *reb__ah__-Hass,* *leekee-dath-y__o__n* |
| **shoe repairer's** | reparación del calzado | *reparath-y__o__n del k__a__lth__ah__-doh* |
| **shoe store** | la zapatería | *thapateh-r__ee__-a* |
| **souvenir store** | la tienda de regalos | *ty__e__nda deh reg__ah__-loss* |
| **sports equipment** | equipos de deporte | *eh-k__ee__poss deh dehp__o__rteh* |
| **sportswear** | ropa de deporte | *r__o__h-pa deh dehp__o__rteh* |
| **stationery store** | la papelería | *papeh-leh-r__ee__-a* |
| **store** | la tienda | *ty__e__nda* |
| **supermarket** | el supermercado | *sooper-mair-k__ah__-doh* |
| **tailor** | la sastrería | *sastreh-r__ee__-a* |
| **tobacco shop** | el estanco | *est__a__nkoh* |
| **toy store** | la juguetería | *Hoo-gheh-teh-r__ee__-a* |
| **travel agency** | la agencia de viajes | *aH__e__nth-ya deh* |
| **women's wear** | señoras | *sen-y__o__rass* *vy__ah__-Hess* |

**Excuse me, where is/are …?** *(in a supermarket)*
Por favor, ¿dónde está/están …?
*por fa-v__o__r d__o__ndeh est__a__/est__a__n*

**Where is there a … (store)?**
¿Dónde hay una (tienda de) …?
*d__o__ndeh I __oo__na ty__e__nda deh*

**Where is the … department?**
¿Dónde está la sección de …?
*d__o__ndeh est__a__ la sekth-y__o__n deh*

**Where is the main shopping area?**
¿Dónde está la zona comercial?
*d__o__ndeh est__a__ la th__o__na kommairth-y__a__l*

**Is there a market here?**
¿Hay algún mercado aquí?
*I algoon mair-kah-doh akee*

**I'd like …**
Quería …
*keh-ree-a*

**Do you have …?**
¿Tienen …?
*tyeh-nen*

**How much is this?**
¿Cuánto es esto?
*kwantoh ess estoh*

**Where do I pay?**
¿Dónde se paga?
*dondeh seh pah-ga*

**Do you take credit cards?**
¿Puedo pagar con tarjeta de crédito?
*pweh-doh pagar kon tar-Heh-ta deh kredeetoh*

**I think perhaps you've shortchanged me**
Me parece que me ha dado cambio de menos
*meh pareh-theh keh meh a dadoh kamb-yoh deh menoss*

**Can I have a receipt?**
¿Me da un recibo?
*meh da oon retheeboh*

**Can I have a bag, please?**
¿Me da una bolsa, por favor?
*meh da oona bolsa por fa-vor*

**I'm just looking**
Sólo estoy mirando
*soh-loh estoy meerandoh*

**I'll come back later**
Volveré luego
*bolvereh lwehgoh*

**Do you have any more of these?**
¿Tiene alguno más de éstos?
*tyeh-neh algoonoh mass deh estoss*

**Do you have anything less expensive?**
¿Tiene usted algo más barato?
*tyeh-neh oosteh algoh mass barah-toh*

**Do you have anything larger/smaller?**
¿Tiene usted algo más grande/pequeño?
*tyeh-neh oosteh algoh mass grandeh/peh-kayn-yoh*

**Can I try it (them) on?**
¿Puedo probármelo(s)?
*pweh-doh probarmeh-loh(ss)*

**Does it come in other colors?**
¿Lo hay en otros colores?
*loh i en otross koloress*

**Could you gift wrap it for me?**
¿Podría envolvérmelo para regalo?
*podree-a embol-vairmeh-loh parra regah-loh*

**I'd like to exchange this, it doesn't work**
Quiero que me cambien esto porque tiene un defecto
*kyeh-roh keh meh kambyen estoh por-keh tyeh-neh oon defektoh*

**I'm afraid I don't have the receipt**
Me temo que no tengo el recibo
*meh temoh keh noh teng-goh el reseeboh*

**Can I have a refund?**
¿Pueden devolverme el dinero?
*pweh-den deh-volvair-meh el deeneh-roh*

**My camera isn't working**
Mi cámara no funciona
*mee kam-eh-ra noh foonth-yoh-na*

**I want a roll of 36-exposure color film. 100 ISO**
Quiero un carrete en color de treinta y seis fotos. De cien ISO
*kyeh-roh oon karreh-teh en kolor deh traynti sayss fotos deh thyen ee esseh oh*

**I'd like this film developed**
Quería revelar este carrete
*kehree-a revelar esteh karreh-teh*

**Matte prints**
Copias en papel mate
*koh-pyass en pappell mateh*

**Glossy prints**
Copias con brillo
*koh-pyass kon bree-yoh*

**One-hour service, please**
Servicio de una hora, por favor
*sairveeth-yoh deh oona ora por fa-vor*

**Where can I get this fixed?**
¿Dónde me pueden arreglar esto?
*dondeh meh pweh-den arreh-glar estoh*

**Can you fix this?**
¿Puede arreglarme esto?
*pweh-deh arrehglarmeh estoh*

**I'd like this skirt/these pants dry-cleaned**
Quiero que me limpien esta falda/estos pantalones
*kyeh-roh keh meh leempyen esta falda/estoss pantaloh-ness*

**When will it (they) be ready?**
¿Cuándo estará(n) listo(s)?
*kwandoh estara(n) leestoh(ss)*

**I'd like some change for the washing machine/dryer**
¿Me puede cambiar dinero para la lavadora/secadora?
*meh pweh-deh kambyar deeneh-roh parra la lavadora/sekadora*

**Can you help me work the machine, please?**
¿Puede enseñarme a manejar la máquina, por favor?
*pweh-deh ensen-yarmeh a maneh-Har la makeena por fa-vor*

**I'd like to make an appointment**
Quería pedir hora
*keh-ree-a pedeer ora*

**I want a cut and blow-dry**
Quería un corte y moldeado con secador de mano
*keh-ree-a oon korteh ee moldeh-ah-doh kon sekador deh mah-noh*

**With conditioner/No conditioner, thanks**
Con acondicionador/Sin acondicionador, por favor
*kon akondeeth-yonador/seen akondeeth-yonador por fa-vor*

**Just a trim, please**
Recórtemelo un poco solamente, por favor
*rekorteh-meh-loh oon pokoh sola-menteh por fa-vor*

**A bit more off here, please**
Córtemelo un poco más por aquí, por favor
*korteh-meh-loh oon pokoh mass por akee por fa-vor*

**Not too much off!**
¡No me corte demasiado!
*noh meh korteh demass-yah-doh*

**When does the market open?**
¿Cuándo se abre el mercado?
*kwandoh seh ah-breh el mair-kah-doh*

**What's the price per kilo?**
¿Cuánto vale el kilo?
*kwantoh valeh el keeloh*

**Could you write that down?**
¿Puede escribírmelo?
*pweh-deh eskreebeermeh-loh*

**That's too much! I'll pay …**
¡Eso es demasiado! Le doy …
*esso ess deh-mass-yah-doh! leh doy*

**I've seen that on another stall for … euros**
Lo he visto en otro puesto a … euros
*loh eh veestoh en otroh pwestoh a … eoo-ros*

**That's fine. I'll take it**
Está bien. Me lo llevo
*esta byen. meh loh yeh-voh*

**I'll have a piece of that cheese**
Quiero un trozo de ese queso
*kyeh-roh oon troh-thoh deh esseh keh-soh*

**About 250/500 grams**
Como doscientos cincuenta/quinientos gramos
*koh-moh dossthyentoss theen-kwenta/keenyentoss grah-moss*

**A kilo/half a kilo of apples, please**
Un kilo/medio kilo de manzanas, por favor
*oon keeloh/meh-dyoh keeloh deh manthah-nass por fa-vor*

**A quarter of a kilo of ham, please**
Un cuarto de kilo de jamón, por favor
*oon kwartoh deh keeloh deh Hamon por fa-vor*

**May I taste it?**
¿Puedo probarlo?
*pweh-doh probarloh*

**No, I don't like it**
No, no me gusta
*noh noh meh goosta*

**That's very nice. I'll take some**
Está muy bueno. Me llevaré un poco
*esta mwee bweh-noh. meh yehvareh oon poh-koh*

**It isn't what I wanted**
No es lo que yo quería
*noh ess loh keh yoh keh-ree-a*

---

### THINGS YOU'LL SEE

| | |
|---|---|
| abierto | open |
| agencia de viajes | travel agency |
| alimentación | groceries |
| alquiler | rental |
| autoservicio | self-service |
| barato | inexpensive |
| barbería | barber |
| bricolage | do-it-yourself supplies |
| caballeros | menswear |
| caja | cash register, checkout |
| calidad | quality |
| calzados | shoe store |
| carnicería | butcher's |
| cerrado | closed |
| cerrado por vacaciones | closed for holidays |
| cerramos los ... | closed on ... |
| droguería | household cleaning materials |
| estanco | tobacco shop |
| ferretería | hardware store |
| flores | flowers |
| ganga | bargain |
| grandes almacenes | department store |
| helados | ice cream parlor |
| juguetes | toys |
| lavado | shampoo, cleaning |

$\longrightarrow$

| | |
|---|---|
| librería | bookstore |
| liquidación total | stock clearance |
| moda | fashion |
| moldeado con secador de mano | blow-dry |
| no se admiten devoluciones | no refunds given |
| no tocar | do not touch |
| objetos de escritorio | office supplies |
| oferta | special offer |
| panadería | bakery |
| papelería | stationery store |
| pastelería | pastry shop |
| peletería | furrier |
| peluquería de caballeros | men's hairstylist |
| peluquería de señoras | women's salon |
| planta sótano | basement floor |
| planta superior | upper floor |
| por favor, use una cesta/un carrito | please take a basket/cart |
| precio | price |
| rebajado | reduced |
| rebajas | sales |
| rebajas de verano | summer sale |
| saldos | sales |
| salón de peluquería | hair salon |
| sección | department |
| señoras | women's department |
| verduras | vegetables |

## THINGS YOU'LL HEAR

**¿Le están atendiendo?**
Are you being served?

**¿Qué desea?**
Can I help you?

**¿No tiene cambio?**
Do you have anything smaller? (money)

**Lo siento, se nos han terminado**
I'm sorry, we're out of stock

**Esto es todo lo que tenemos**
This is all we have

**No podemos devolver el importe**
We cannot give cash refunds

**¿Desea algo más?**
Will there be anything else?

**¿Cuánto quería?**
How much would you like?

**¿Le importa que sea un poco más?**
Does it matter if it's a bit over?

**Lo siento, no admitimos tarjetas de crédito**
I'm afraid we don't take credit cards

**¿Cómo quiere que se lo corte?**
How would you like it cut?

# SPORTS

Thanks to Spain's excellent climate, almost all outdoor sports
are well represented. The east and south coasts especially
provide excellent opportunities for swimming, water-skiing,
sailing, fishing (including underwater fishing), and
sailboarding. The north coast also has good facilities and is
becoming more and more popular, despite the cooler climate.
A flag warning system operates on most Atlantic beaches: red
for dangerous conditions, yellow for caution, and green for all
clear. Renting equipment is no problem, and everything from a
beach umbrella to a sailboard is offered at a reasonable charge.
Golf, which has become very popular, is played all year round,
and there are courses in Madrid and nearly all the major beach
resorts. Most golf courses offer lessons. Tennis courts can be
found in most places and squash is gaining in popularity.
Bicycling is very popular, and there are now more and more
places where you can rent bicycles. In areas such as the
Pyrenees and the Sierra Nevada, there is mountaineering,
walking, and skiing in the winter.

## USEFUL WORDS AND PHRASES

| | | |
|---|---|---|
| **athletics** | el atletismo | *atleh-teezmoh* |
| **badminton** | el badminton | *badmeen-ton* |
| **ball** | la pelota | *peh-loh-ta* |
| **beginners' slope** | la pista de principiantes | *peesta deh preentheepyantess* |
| **bicycle** | una bicicleta | *beethee-kleh-ta* |
| **bicycle path** | el carril para bicicletas | *karreel parra beetheekleh-tass* |
| **bicycling** | el ciclismo | *theekleezmoh* |
| **binding** (*ski*) | una atadura | *atadoora* |
| **bullfighting** | los toros | *toh-ross* |
| **canoe** | una piragua | *peerah-gwa* |
| **canoeing** | el piragüismo | *peerag-weezmoh* |
| **cross-country skiing** | el esquí de fondo | *eskee deh fondoh* |

| current | una corriente | korry*e*nteh |
| dive | tirarse de cabeza | teer*a*rseh deh kab*e*h-tha |
| diving board | un trampolín | trampoh-l*ee*n |
| fishing | la pesca | p*e*ska |
| fishing rod | una caña de pescar | k*a*hn-ya deh pesk*a*r |
| flippers | las aletas | al*e*h-tass |
| game | un juego | Hw*e*h-goh |
| goggles | las gafas de bucear | g*a*h-fass deh booth*e*h-*a*r |
| golf | el golf | golf |
| play golf | jugar al golf | Hoog*a*r al golf |
| golf club (*stick*) | el palo | p*a*loh |
| golf course | un campo de golf | k*a*mpoh deh golf |
| gymnastics | la gimnasia | H*ee*mn*a*ss-ya |
| hang gliding | el ala delta | *a*la d*e*lta |
| harpoon | el fusil submarino | foo-s*ee*l soobma-r*ee*noh |
| go hiking | hacer senderismo | ath*ai*r sendair*ee*zmoh |
| hockey | el hockey | H*o*kkay |
| hunting | la caza | k*a*tha |
| mast | el mástil | m*a*steel |
| mountaineering | el montañismo | montan-y*ee*zmoh |
| oxygen bottles | las botellas de oxígeno | bot*ay*-yass deh oks*ee*-Hennoh |
| paragliding | el parapente | parap*e*nteh |
| pedal boat | un hidropedal | eedroh-peh-d*a*l |
| piste | la pista | p*ee*sta |
| Pyrenees | los Pirineos | peereen*e*h-oss |
| racket | una raqueta | rak*e*h-ta |
| ride | montar a caballo | mont*a*r a kab*a*-yoh |
| riding | la equitación | ekeetath-y*o*n |
| riding hat | el casco de equitación | k*a*skoh deh ekeetath-y*o*n |
| rock climbing | el alpinismo | alpeen*ee*zmoh |
| saddle | la silla | s*ee*-ya |
| sail (*noun*) | la vela | v*e*h-la |
| (*verb*) | navegar (a vela) | naveg*a*r a v*e*h-la |
| sailboard | una tabla de windsurfing | t*a*h-bla deh weends*oo*rfeen |

| | | |
|---|---|---|
| sailing | vela | *veh-la* |
| go sailing | hacer vela | *athair veh la* |
| skate *(verb)* | patinar | *pateenar* |
| skates | los patines | *patee-ness* |
| skating rink | la pista de patinaje | *peesta deh pateenah-Heh* |
| ski *(noun)* | un esquí | *eskee* |
| *(verb)* | esquiar | *eskyar* |
| ski boots | las botas de esquí | *botass deh eskee* |
| skiing | el esquí | *eskee* |
| ski lift | el telesquí | *tehlehskee* |
| skin diving | el submarinismo | *soobmaree-neezmoh* |
| ski pass | un abono | *aboh-noh* |
| ski poles | los bastones | *bastoh-ness* |
| ski tow | el remonte | *remonteh* |
| ski trail | la pista de fondo | *peesta deh fondoh* |
| ski wax | la cera de esquís | *theh-ra deh eskeess* |
| sled | el trineo | *treeneh-oh* |
| snorkel | el respirador | *resspeera-dor* |
| soccer ball | el balón | *ba-lon* |
| soccer match | un partido de fútbol | *partee-doh deh foot-bol* |
| sports center | el polideportivo | *poleedeporteevoh* |
| stadium | el estadio | *estah-dyoh* |
| surfboard | la tabla de surfing | *tabla deh soorfeen* |
| swim | nadar | *nadar* |
| swimming pool | la piscina | *peessthee-na* |
| team | el equipo | *ekeepoh* |
| tennis | el tenis | *teh-neess* |
| tennis court | una pista de tenis | *peesta deh teh-neess* |
| tennis racket | una raqueta de tenis | *rakeh-ta deh teh-neess* |
| toboggan | el tobogán | *tobogan* |
| underwater fishing | la pesca submarina | *peska soobmaree-na* |
| volleyball | el vóleibol | *vollay-bol* |
| water-skiing | el esquí acuático | *eskee akwatee-koh* |
| water skis | los esquís acuáticos | *eskeess akwatee-koss* |

| | | |
|---|---|---|
| **wet suit** | un traje isotérmico | *trah-Heh eessoh-* |
| | | *tairmee-koh* |
| **go windsurfing** | hacer windsurfing | *athair weendsoorfeen* |
| **yacht** | un yate | *yah-teh* |

**How do I get to the beach?**
¿Por dónde se va a la playa?
*por dondeh seh va a la pla-ya*

**How deep is the water here?**
¿Qué profundidad tiene el agua aquí?
*keh profoondee-da tyeh-neh el ah-gwa akee*

**Is there an indoor/outdoor pool here?**
¿Hay piscina cubierta/al aire libre aquí?
*I peessthee-na koob-yairta/al I-reh leebreh akee*

**Is it safe to swim here?**
¿Se puede nadar sin peligro aquí?
*seh pweh-deh nadar seen pelee-groh akee*

**Can I fish here?**
¿Puedo pescar aquí?
*pweh-doh peskar akee*

**Do I need a license?**
¿Necesito un permiso?
*nethessee-toh oon pair-meessoh*

**Is there a golf course near here?**
¿Hay algún campo de golf por aquí cerca?
*I algoon kampoh deh golf por akee thairka*

**Do I have to be a member?**
¿Es necesario ser socio?
*ess nethessaryoh sair soh-thyoh*

**I would like to rent a bicycle/some skis**
Quería alquilar una bicicleta/unos esquís
*keh-ree-a alkee-lar oona beethee-kleh-ta/oonoss eskees*

**How much does it cost per hour/day?**
¿Cuánto cuesta por hora/por día?
*kwantoh kwesta por ora/por dee-a*

**I would like to take water-skiing lessons**
Quería dar clases de esquí acuático
*keh-ree-a dar klah-sess deh eskee akwatee-koh*

**Where can I rent …?**
¿Dónde puedo alquilar …?
*dondeh pweh-doh alkee-lar*

**There's something wrong with this binding**
No sé qué pasa con esta atadura
*noh seh keh pah-sa kon esta atadoora*

**How much is a weekly pass for the ski lift?**
¿Cuánto valen los abonos semanales para el telesquí?
*kwantoh balen loss aboh-noss semanah-less parra el tehlehskee*

**What are the snow conditions like today?**
¿Cuál es el estado de la nieve hoy?
*kwal ess el estadoh deh la nyeh-veh oy*

**I'd like to try cross-country skiing**
Me gustaría probar el esquí de fondo
*meh goostaree-a probar el eskee deh fondoh*

**I haven't played this before**
Nunca había jugado a esto antes
*noonka abee-a Hoogah-doh a estoh antess*

**Let's go skating/swimming**
Vamos a patinar/nadar
*bah-moss a pateenar/nadar*

**What's the score?**
¿A cómo van?
*a koh-moh van*

**Who won?**
¿Quién ha ganado?
*kyen a ganadoh*

## THINGS YOU'LL SEE

| | |
|---|---|
| **acceso playa** | to the beach |
| **alquiler de barcos** | boat rental |
| **alquiler de bicicletas** | bike rental |
| **alquiler de esquís** | (water) ski rental |
| **alquiler de sombrillas** | umbrella rental |
| **alquiler de tablas** | board rental |
| **alquiler de tumbonas** | lounge chair rental |
| **camino privado** | private entrance |
| **campo de golf** | golf course |
| **corriente peligrosa** | dangerous current |
| **palos de golf** | golf clubs |
| **peatones** | pedestrians |
| **peligro** | danger |
| **piscina** | swimming pool |
| **piscina cubierta** | indoor swimming pool |
| **pista de tenis** | tennis court |
| **prohibido bañarse** | no swimming |
| **prohibido el paso** | no trespassing |
| **prohibido encender fuego** | no fires |
| **prohibido pescar** | no fishing |
| **remonte** | ski tow |
| **socorrista** | lifeguard |
| **telecabina** | cable car |
| **telesilla** | chair lift |
| **telesquí** | ski lift |

# POST OFFICES AND BANKS

Post offices in Spain deal only with mail, so don't look for a phone there. Use a phone booth or find the exchange (**Telefónica**). Stamps can be bought in the post office, but most Spaniards go to an **estanco** (a state tobacco shop—look for the brown and yellow sign) where you can also buy postcards. Mailboxes are yellow.

   Banks are open half a day, usually from 9 AM to 1:30 PM Monday to Friday, although this may vary depending on where you are. They are also open on Saturdays until 1 PM. There are usually only one or two cashiers. First you have to go to the foreign exchange counter, **cambio**, and then line up for the cashier. However, more and more banks in large towns are changing over to the system where all transactions take place at the same counter. ATMs are widespread.

   The Spanish unit of currency is the common European currency, the **euro** (*eoo-roh*). One **euro** is divided into 100 **céntimos** (*thentimos*), and the coins come in 1, 2, 5, 10, 20, and 50 **céntimos**; 1 and 2 **euros**. Bills are available in 5, 10, 20, 50, 100, 200, and 500 **euros**.

## USEFUL WORDS AND PHRASES

| | | |
|---|---|---|
| **airmail** | correo aéreo | *korreh-oh ah-aireh-oh* |
| **ATM** | el cajero automático | *kah-Heroh owtomateekoh* |
| **bank** | el banco | *bankoh* |
| **bill, bank note** | un billete de banco | *bee-yehteh deh bankoh* |
| **cash** | dinero en efectivo | *deeneroh en efekteevoh* |
| **change** (*verb*) | cambiar | *kambyar* |
| **check** | un cheque | *cheh-keh* |
| **checkbook** | el talonario de cheques | *talonaryoh deh cheh-kehss* |
| **collection** | la recogida | *reh-koh-Heeda* |
| **counter** | el mostrador | *mostrador* |

| | | |
|---|---|---|
| credit card | la tarjeta de crédito | *tar-Heh-ta deh kredeetoh* |
| customs form | el impreso para la aduana | *eempreh-soh parra la adwah-na* |
| delivery | el reparto | *reh-partoh* |
| deposit (*noun*) | un ingreso | *eengreh-soh* |
| (*verb*) | ingresar | *eengreh-sar* |
| dollar | el dólar | *dohlar* |
| exchange rate | el tipo de cambio | *teepoh deh kambyoh* |
| fax (*noun*) | un fax | *fax* |
| (*verb: document*) | mandar por fax | *mandar por fax* |
| fax machine | el fax | *fax* |
| form | un impreso | *eempreh-soh* |
| general delivery | la lista de correos | *leesta deh korreh-oss* |
| international money order | un giro internacional | *Heeroh eentairnath-yonal* |
| letter | una carta | *karta* |
| letter carrier | el cartero | *karteh-roh* |
| mail (*noun*) | el correo | *korreh-oh* |
| (*verb*) | echar al buzón | *etchar al boothon* |
| mailbox | el buzón | *boothon* |
| money order | un giro (postal) | *Hee-roh postal* |
| package/parcel | un paquete | *pakeh-teh* |
| postage rates | las tarifas postales | *tarree-fass postah-less* |
| postcard | una postal | *postal* |
| post office | (la oficina de) correos | *offee-theena deh korreh-oss* |
| registered letter | una carta certificada | *karta thair-teefee-kah-da* |
| stamp | un sello | *say-yoh* |
| surface mail | correo ordinario | *korreh-oh ordee-nar-yoh* |
| traveler's check | un cheque de viaje | *cheh-keh deh vyah-Heh* |
| withdraw | retirar/sacar | *reteerar/sakar* |
| withdrawal | una retirada | *reteerah-da* |
| zip code | el distrito | *deestree-toh postal* |

**How much is a letter/postcard to …**
¿Qué franqueo lleva una carta/una postal a …
keh fran-_keh_-oh _yeh_-va _oo_na _ka_rta/_oo_na post_al_ a

**I would like three 45 cent stamps**
Quería tres sellos de cuarenta y cinco céntimos
keh-_ree_-a tress _say_-yoss deh kwar_en_tı _theen_koh th_en_timos

**I want to register this letter**
Quiero mandar esta carta certificada
kee-_eh_-roh mand_ar e_sta _ka_rta thair-teefee-_kah_-da

**I want to send this package to …**
Quiero mandar este paquete a …
kee-_eh_-roh mand_ar e_steh pak_eh_-teh a

**How long does the mail to … take?**
¿Cuánto tarda el correo para …?
kw_an_toh t_a_rda el korr_eh_-oh p_a_rra

**Where can I mail this?**
¿Dónde puedo echar esto?
d_on_deh pw_eh_-doh etch_a_r e_s_toh

**Is there any mail for me?**
¿Hay algún correo para mí?
i alg_oo_n korr_eh_-oh p_a_rra mee

**I'd like to send a fax**
Quería mandar un fax
keh-_ree_-a mand_a_r oon fax

**This is to go airmail**
Esto quiero que vaya por avión
_e_stoh kee-_eh_-roh keh v_a_-ya por av-y_on_

**I'd like to change this into euros**
Quiero cambiar esto en euros
kee-_eh_-roh kamby_a_r _e_stoh en _eoo_-ros

**Can I cash these traveler's checks?**
Quisiera hacer efectivos estos cheques de viaje
*keesy_e_ra ath_ai_r efekt_ee_voss _e_stoss ch_eh_-kess deh vy_ah_-Heh*

**What is the exchange rate for the dollar?**
¿A cuánto está el dólar?
*a kw_a_ntoh est_a_ el d_o_hlar*

**Can I draw cash using this credit card?**
¿Puedo sacar dinero con esta tarjeta (de crédito)?
*pw_eh_-doh sak_a_r deen_e_roh kon _e_sta tar-H_eh_-ta deh kr_e_deetoh*

**I'd like it in 20 euro bills**
¿Me lo puede dar en billetes de veinte euros, por favor?
*meh loh pw_eh_-deh dar en bee-y_eh_-tess deh v_a_ynteh _eoo_-ros por fa-v_o_r*

**Could you give me smaller bills?**
¿Podría darme billetes más pequeños?
*podr_ee_-a d_a_rmeh bee-y_eh_-tess mas peh-k_eh_-nyoss*

---

### THINGS YOU'LL SEE

| | |
|---|---|
| banco | bank |
| buzón | mailbox |
| caja | cashier |
| cajero automático | ATM |
| cambio (de divisas) | currency exchange |
| cartas | letters |
| certificados | registered mail |
| correo aéreo | airmail |
| correo urgente | express |
| cuentas corrientes | checking accounts |
| destinatario | addressee |
| dirección | address |
| distrito postal | zip code |
| España | Spain (domestic postage) |
| extranjero | postage abroad |

→

| | |
|---|---|
| franqueo | postage |
| giros | money orders |
| horas de oficina | opening hours |
| horas de recogida | collection times |
| ingresos | deposits |
| lista de correos | general delivery |
| localidad | place |
| mercado de divisas | exchange rates |
| paquetes | packages |
| postal | postcard |
| rellenar | to fill in |
| remitente | sender |
| sello | stamp |
| tarifa | charge |
| venta de sellos | stamps |

# COMMUNICATIONS

*Telephones:* Telephone booths in Spain are blue. They take coins of 10 cents, 20 cents, 50 cents, 1 euro, and 2 euros as well as phonecards which are far more convenient and can be bought at newsstands and **estancos**. Some phones are equipped with multilingual electronic instruction displays.

To call the US, dial 07 and wait for a high-pitched tone, then dial 1 followed by the area code and the number you want.

The tones you hear on Spanish phones when making a call within Spain differ slightly from ours:

| | |
|---|---|
| Dial tone: | same as in US |
| Ringing: | repeated long tone |
| Busy signal: | rapid beeps |

There are also payphones in bars and restaurants, some of which have phones with a counter that is set to zero when you begin a call. Alternatively, you can look for the **central telefónica** or **teléfonos** (telephone exchange) that are located in the center of most towns. Run by **Telefónica** (look for the logo, standing for Spain's national telephone company), these are sometimes open 24 hours a day in major towns. You ask the cashier for the number you want, and then go to a booth and wait for the call to be put through. You pay when you have finished your call. Another sign to look for is **locutorio telefónico**, where you'll find telephone booths that operate the same system as the **central telefónica** and that are located near the beach in main resorts. There are also private **locutorios** in major towns which, although they can be more expensive, could save you a long trek to the **central telefónica**.

## USEFUL WORDS AND PHRASES

| | | |
|---|---|---|
| **call** (*noun*) | una llamada | *yamah-da* |
| (*verb*) | llamar | *yamar* |
| **cardphone** | un teléfono con uso de tarjeta | *teh-leffonoh kon oosoh deh tar-Heh-ta* |

| code | el prefijo | *preh-fee-Hoh* |
|---|---|---|
| collect call | una llamada a cobro revertido | *yamah-da a kobroh reh-vair-teedoh* |
| dial | marcar | *markar* |
| dial tone | la señal para marcar | *sen-yal parra markar* |
| email address | la dirección de email | *deerektheeon deh eemail* |
| emergency | una emergencia | *emmair-Henth-ya* |
| extension | extensión | *ekstenth-yon* |
| fax machine | el fax | *fax* |
| information | información | *eenformath-yon* |
| internet | el internet | *internet* |
| international | internacional | *eentair-nath-yonal* |
| mobile phone | el teléfono móvil | *teh-leffonoh mohbeel* |
| number | el número | *noomeh-roh* |
| operator | la operadora | *opeh-radora* |
| payphone | un teléfono público | *teh-leffonoh poobleekoh* |
| phone booth | una cabina telefónica | *kabeena tehleh-fonnika* |
| phonecard | una tarjeta de teléfono | *tar-Heh-ta deh teh-leffonoh* |
| phone book | la guía telefónica | *gee-a tehleh-fonnika* |
| photocopier | la fotocopiadora | *fotokopeeadora* |
| receiver | el aparato | *aparah-toh* |
| telephone | un teléfono | *teh-leffonoh* |
| touch-tone phone | un teléfono automático | *teh-leffonoh owtoh-matikoh* |
| website | la web site | *'web site'* |
| wrong number | el número equivocado | *noomeh-roh eh-keevoh-kah-doh* |

**Where is the nearest phone booth?**
¿Dónde está la cabina telefónica más cercana?
*dondeh esta la kabeena tehleh-fonnika mass thair-kah-na*

**Is there a phone book?**
¿Hay una guía telefónica?
*I oona gee-a tehleh-fonnika*

**How much is a call to America?**
¿Cuánto cuesta una llamada a América?
*kwantoh kwesta oona yamah-da a amairika*

**I would like to make a collect call**
Quiero que sea a cobro revertido
*kyeh-roh keh seh-a a koh-broh reh-vair-teedoh*

**I would like a number in Barcelona**
Quiero un número de Barcelona
*kyeh-roh oon noomeh-roh deh bartheh-lohna*

**Could you give me an outside line?**
¿Puede darme línea, por favor?
*pweh-deh dar-meh leeneh-a por fa-vor*

**How do I get an outside line?**
¿Cómo puedo obtener línea?
*koh-moh pweh-doh obtenair leeneh-a*

**Hello, this is … speaking**
Hola, soy …
*oh-la soy*

**Is that …?**
¿Es (usted) …?
*ess oosteh*

**Hello** (*when answering*)
Dígame
*dee-gah-meh*

**Speaking**
Al habla
*al abla*

**I would like to speak to …**
Quería hablar con …
*keh-ree-a ablar kon*

**Extension …, please**
Extensión …, por favor
*ekstenss-yon … por fa-vor*

**Please tell him/her … called**
Haga el favor de decirle que ha llamado …
*ah-ga el fa-vor deh deh-theerleh keh a yamah-doh*

**Would you ask him/her to call me back, please**
Dígale que me llame cuando vuelva
*dee-gah-leh keh meh yah-meh kwandoh vwelva*

**Do you know where he/she is?**
¿Sabe usted dónde está?
*sah-beh oosteh dondeh esta*

**When will he/she be back?**
¿Cuándo volverá?
*kwandoh volveh-ra*

**Could you leave him/her a message?**
¿Podría dejarle un recado?
*podree-a deh-Harleh oon reh-kah-doh*

**I'll call back later**
Volveré a llamar luego
*volveh-reh a yamar lweh-goh*

**Sorry, I've got the wrong number**
Lo siento, me he equivocado de número
*loh syen-toh meh eh ekeevoh-kah-doh deh noomeh-roh*

**What's your fax number/email address?**
¿Cual es su número de fax/dirección de email?
*kwal ess soo noomeh-roh deh fax/deerektheeon de eemail*

**Did you get my fax/email?**
¿Recibió mi fax/email?
*retheebeeoh mee fax/eemail*

**Please resend your fax**
Por favor, envíe de nuevo su fax
*por favor enbee-eh de nooebo soo fax*

**Can I use the photocopier/fax machine?**
¿Puedo usar la fotocopiadora/el fax
*pweh-doh oosar la fotokopeeadora/el fax*

---

### THE ALPHABET

| | | | | | | | |
|---|---|---|---|---|---|---|---|
| a | *ah* | g | *Heh* | n | *eneh* | t | *teh* |
| b | *beh* | h | *acheh* | ñ | *enyeh* | u | *oo* |
| c | *theh* | i | *ee* | o | *o* | v | *oobeh* |
| ch | *cheh* | j | *Hota* | p | *peh* | w | *oobeh dobleh* |
| d | *deh* | k | *ka* | q | *koo* | x | *ekiss* |
| e | *eh* | l | *eleh* | r | *ereh* | y | *ee gryehga* |
| f | *efeh* | m | *emeh* | s | *eseh* | z | *thehta* |

---

### THINGS YOU'LL SEE

| | |
|---|---|
| **cabina telefónica** | telephone booth |
| **central telefónica** | telephone exchange |
| **descolgar el aparato** | lift receiver |
| **Estados Unidos (EEUU)** | US |
| **fax** | fax machine |
| **fotocopiadora** | photocopier |
| **guía telefónica** | telephone book |
| **insertar monedas** | insert coins |
| **interurbana** | long-distance |
| **llamada** | call |
| **locutorio telefónico** | telephone booth |

→

| marcar el número | dial the number |
| monedas | coins |
| no funciona | out of order |
| número | number |
| operadora | operator |
| páginas amarillas | Yellow Pages |
| paso (de contador) | unit |
| prefijo | area code |
| reparaciones | repair service |
| servicio a través de operadora | dialing through the operator |
| servicio automático | direct dialing |
| sitio web | website |
| tarifa | charges |
| tarjeta telefónica | phonecard |
| Telefónica | Spanish national telephone company |
| teléfono móvil | mobile phone |
| urbana | local |
| web site | website |

## THINGS YOU'LL HEAR

**¿A dónde quiere llamar?**
Where do you want to call?

**Vaya a la cabina cuatro**
Now go to booth number 4

**¿Con quién quiere que le ponga?**
Whom would you like to speak to?

**Se ha equivocado de número**
You've got the wrong number

**¿Quién es?**
Who's speaking?

→

**Al aparato/Al habla/Soy yo**
Speaking

**Diga/Dígame**
Hello

**¿Cuál es su teléfono?**
What is your number?

**Lo siento, no está**
Sorry, he/she's not in

**Puede dejar un recado**
You can leave a message

**Volverá dentro de … minutos/horas**
He'll/she'll be back in … minutes/hours

**Vuelva a llamar mañana, por favor**
Please call again tomorrow

**Le diré que le/la ha llamado usted**
I'll tell him/her you called

**Las líneas con Sevilla se encuentran ocupadas en este momento. Repita la llamada dentro de unos minutos.**
All lines to Seville are busy at the moment. Please call again in a few minutes' time.

**Le pongo/paso con …**
I'll put you through…

# EMERGENCIES

Information on local health services can be obtained from tourist information offices, but in an emergency dial **091** for the police. They will put you through to the ambulance service or fire department, since there is no national central number for these emergency services.

In case of sudden illness or accident, go to the nearest **casa de socorro** (emergency first-aid center) or to an **urgencias** (hospital emergency room). If on the road, look for **puestos de socorro**, which is also an emergency first-aid center.

In the event of your car breaking down, try to get to the nearest **taller** (garage) or, if this is not possible, to the nearest service station, where they will be able to advise you on whom to phone. If you are a member of AAA, there is a reciprocal agreement with the **RACE** (**Real Automóvil Club de España**) under which you should be covered.

## USEFUL WORDS AND PHRASES

| | | |
|---|---|---|
| accident | un accidente | *akthee-denteh* |
| ambulance | una ambulancia | *amboolanth-ya* |
| assault | agredir | *agreh-deer* |
| breakdown | una avería | *aveh-ree-a* |
| break down (verb) | tener una avería | *tenair oona aveh-ree-a* |
| burglar | un ladrón | *ladron* |
| burglary | un robo | *roh-boh* |
| crash | un accidente | *akthee-denteh* |
| emergency | una emergencia | *emair-henth-ya* |
| emergency room | urgencias | *oor-henth-yass* |
| fire | un fuego | *fwehgoh* |
| (large) | un incendio | *eenthend-yoh* |
| fire department | los bomberos | *bombeh-ross* |
| flood | una inundación | *eenoondath-yon* |
| injured | herido | *ereedoh* |
| pickpocket | un carterista | *kartereesta* |

| police | la policía | *poleethee-a* |
|---|---|---|
| police station | la comisaria | *kommeessaree-a* |
| theft | un robo | *rohboh* |
| thief | un ladrón | *ladron* |
| tow | remolcar | *remolkar* |
| towing service | servicio de grúa | *saitveeth yoh deh groo-a* |

**Help!**
¡Socorro!
*sokorroh*

**Look out!**
¡Cuidado!
*kweedah-doh*

**Stop!**
¡Pare!
*pareh*

**This is an emergency!**
¡Esto es una emergencia!
*estoh ess oona emair-нenth-ya*

**Get an ambulance!**
¡Llame a una ambulancia!
*yah-meh a oona amboolanth-ya*

**Hurry up!**
¡Dése prisa!
*deh-seh preessa*

**Please send an ambulance to …**
Mande una ambulancia a …
*mandeh oona amboolanth-ya a*

**Please come to …**
Haga el favor de venir a …
*ah-ga el fa-vor deh veneer a*

**My address is ...**
Mi dirección es ...
*mee deerekth-yon ess*

**We've had a break-in**
Hemos tenido un robo en la casa
*ehmoss teneedoh oon rohboh en la kasa*

**There's a fire at ...**
Hay un fuego en ...
*I oon fwehgoh en*

**Someone's been injured/run over**
Hay una persona herida/atropellada
*I oona pairsona ereeda/atropeh-yah-da*

**He's passed out**
Ha perdido el conocimiento
*a pairdeedoh el konotheemmyentoh*

**My passport/car has been stolen**
Me han robado el pasaporte/el coche
*meh an robah-doh el passaporteh/el kotcheh*

**I've lost my traveler's checks**
He perdido mis cheques de viaje
*eh pairdeedoh meess cheh-kess deh vyah-Heh*

**I want to report a stolen credit card**
Quiero denunciar el robo de una tarjeta de crédito
*kyeh-roh denoonthyar el rohboh deh oona tar-Heh-ta deh kredeetoh*

**It was stolen from my room**
Lo robaron de mi habitación
*lo robah-ron deh mee abeetath-yon*

**I lost it in/at...**
Lo perdí en ...
*lo pairdee en*

**My luggage is missing**
Mi equipaje se ha perdido
*mee ekeepah-Heh seh a pairdeedoh*

**Has my luggage turned up yet?**
¿Ha aparecido ya mi equipaje?
*a apareh-theedoh ya mee ekeepah-Heh*

**I've had a crash**
He tenido un accidente
*eh teneedoh oon akthee-denteh*

**My car's been broken into**
Me han forzado el coche
*meh an forthah-doh el kotcheh*

**The registration number is …**
El número de matrícula es el …
*el noomeroh deh matreekoola ess el*

**I've been mugged**
Me han atacado
*meh an atakah-doh*

**My son's missing**
Mi hijo se ha perdido
*mee ee-Hoh seh a pairdeedo*

**He has fair/brown hair**
Tiene el pelo rubio/moreno
*tyeh-neh el peh-loh roob-yoh/moreh-noh*

**He's … years old**
Tiene … años
*tyeh-neh … ahn-yoss*

**I've locked myself out of my house/room/car**
Me he dejado la llave dentro de la casa/habitación/del coche
*meh eh deh-Hah-doh la yah-veh dentroh deh la kasa/abeetath-yon/ del kotcheh*

**He's drowning**
Se está ahogando
*seh está ah-oh-gandoh*

**She can't swim**
No sabe nadar
*noh sabeh nadar*

---

## THINGS YOU'LL SEE

| | |
|---|---|
| **abierto las 24 horas del día** | 24-hour service |
| **botiquín** | first-aid box |
| **casa de socorro** | emergency first-aid center |
| **comisaría** | police station |
| **farmacia de guardia** | pharmacy on duty |
| **fuego** | fire |
| **guardia civil de tráfico** | traffic police |
| **marque …** | dial … |
| **policía** | police |
| **primeros auxilios** | first-aid center |
| **puesto de socorro** | first-aid center |
| **servicios de rescate** | mountain rescue |
| **socorrista** | lifeguard |
| **taller (de reparaciones)** | garage |
| **urgencias** | emergency room |

---

## THINGS YOU'LL HEAR

**¿Cuál es su dirección?**
What's your address?

**¿Dónde se encuentra usted ahora?**
Where are you?

**¿Puede describirlo/describirle?**
Can you describe it/him?

# HEALTH

Medicines are available only from the **farmacia** (pharmacy), usually open from 9 AM to 1 PM and from 4 PM to 8 PM. If the pharmacy is closed, there will be a notice on the door that gives the address of the **farmacia de guardia**—pharmacy on duty (See Emergencies, page 108.)

## USEFUL WORDS AND PHRASES

| accident | un accidente | akthee-d_e_nteh |
| --- | --- | --- |
| ambulance | una ambulancia | ambool_a_nth-ya |
| anemic | anémico | ann_e_h-meekoh |
| appendicitis | una apendicitis | apendee-th_e_eteess |
| appendix | el apéndice | ap_e_n-deetheh |
| aspirin | una aspirina | asspee-r_e_ena |
| asthma | asma | _a_zma |
| backache | un dolor de espalda | dol_o_r deh essp_a_lda |
| bandage | el vendaje | vend_a_h-нeh |
| bite (by dog) | una mordedura | mordeh-d_oo_ra |
| (by insect) | una picadura | peeka-d_oo_ra |
| bladder | la vejiga | veh-н_e_ega |
| blister | una ampolla | amp_o_h-ya |
| blood | la sangre | s_a_ngreh |
| blood donor | un donante de sangre | doh-n_a_nteh deh s_a_ngreh |
| burn | una quemadura | keh-mad_oo_ra |
| cancer | el cáncer | k_a_nthair |
| cast | la escayola | eskayy_o_h-la |
| chest | el pecho | p_e_h-tchoh |
| chicken pox | la varicela | varee-th_e_h-la |
| cold | un resfriado | resfree-_a_h-doh |
| concussion | una conmoción | konmth-y_o_n |
| constipation | estreñimiento | estren-yeem-y_e_ntoh |
| contact lenses | las lentes de contacto | l_e_ntess deh kont_a_ktoh |

113

| corn | un callo | *kah-yoh* |
|---|---|---|
| cough | tos | *toss* |
| cut | un corte | *korteh* |
| dentist | el dentista | *denteesta* |
| diabetes | la diabetes | *dee-abeh--tess* |
| diarrhea | una diarrea | *dee-arreh-a* |
| dizzy | mareado | *marreh-ah-doh* |
| doctor | el médico | *meddeekoh* |
| earache | un dolor de oídos | *dolor deh oh-eedoss* |
| fever | la fiebre | *fee-eh-breh* |
| filling | un empaste | *empasteh* |
| first aid | primeros auxilios | *preemeh-ross owk-zeel-yoss* |
| flu | la gripe | *greepeh* |
| fracture | una fractura | *fraktoora* |
| German measles | la rubeola | *roobeh-ola* |
| glasses | las gafas | *gah-fass* |
| hangover | una resaca | *resaka* |
| hay fever | la fiebre del heno | *fee-eh-breh del eh-noh* |
| headache | un dolor de cabeza | *dolor deh kabeh-tha* |
| heart | el corazón | *korrathon* |
| heart attack | un infarto | *eemfartoh* |
| hemorrhage | una hemorragia | *emmoraн-hya* |
| hepatitis | la hepatitis | *hehpateetees* |
| HIV positive | seropositivo | *sehrroposeeteeve* |
| hospital | el hospital | *osspeetal* |
| indigestion | una indigestión | *eendee-нest-yon* |
| injection | una inyección | *eenyekth-yon* |
| itch | un picor | *peekor* |
| kidney | el riñón | *reen-yon* |
| lump | un bulto | *booltoh* |
| measles | el sarampión | *saramp-yon* |
| migraine | una jaqueca | *нakeh-ka* |
| motion sickness sickness | mareo | *marreh-oh* |

| mumps | las paperas | *papeh-rass* |
| nausea | náuseas | *now-seh-ass* |
| nurse *(female)* | la enfermera | *enfairmeh-ra* |
| *(male)* | el enfermero | *ennfairmeh-ro* |
| operation | una operación | *oppeh-rath-yon* |
| optician | el oculista | *okooleess-ta* |
| pain | un dolor | *dolor* |
| penicillin | la penicilina | *peneethee-leena* |
| pharmacy | la farmacia | *farmath-ya* |
| pneumonia | una neumonía | *neh-oomonee-a* |
| pregnant | embarazada | *embarra-thah-da* |
| prescription | una receta | *reh-theh-ta* |
| rheumatism | el reúma | *reh-oo-ma* |
| scald | una quemadura | *keh-madoora* |
| scratch | un arañazo | *arran-yah-thoh* |
| sick | enfermo | *emfairmoh* |
| sore throat | un dolor de garganta | *dolor deh garganta* |
| splinter | una astilla | *astee-ya* |
| sprain | una torcedura | *tortheh-doora* |
| sting | una picadura | *peeka-doora* |
| stomach | el estómago | *estoh-magoh* |
| tonsils | las amígdalas | *ameegda-lass* |
| toothache | un dolor de muelas | *dolor deh mweh-lass* |
| ulcer | una úlcera | *ooltheh-ra* |
| vaccination | la vacunación | *vakoonath-yon* |
| vomit | vomitar | *vommee-tar* |
| whooping cough | la tosferina | *tossfeh-reena* |

**I have a pain in …**
Me duele …
*meh dweh-leh*

**I don't feel well**
No me encuentro bien
*noh men enkwen-troh byen*

**I feel faint**
Me encuentro débil
*meh enkwen-troh-deh-beel*

**I feel sick**
Tengo náuseas
*teng-goh now-seh-ass*

**I feel dizzy**
Estoy mareado
*estoy marreh-ah-doh*

**It hurts here**
Me duele aquí
*meh dweh-leh akee*

**It's a sharp pain**
Es un dolor agudo
*ess oon dolor agoodoh*

**It's a dull pain**
Es un dolor leve
*ess oon dolor lehve*

**It hurts all the time**
Es un dolor constante
*ess oon dolor konstanteh*

**It only hurts now and then**
Sólo me duele a ratos
*soloh meh dweh-leh a rah-toss*

**It hurts when you touch it**
Me duele al tocarlo
*meh dweh-leh al tokarloh*

**It hurts more at night**
Me duele más por la noche
*meh dweh-leh mass por la notcheh*

**It stings/It itches**
Me escuece/Me pica
*meh ess-kweh-theh/meh peeka*

**It aches**
Me duele
*meh dweh-leh*

**I have a temperature**
Tengo fiebre
*teng-goh fee-eh-breh*

**I'm … months pregnant**
Estoy embarrazada de … meses
*estoy embarrathahda de … mehses*

**I need a prescription for …**
Necesito una receta para …
*nehtheh-seetoh oona reh-theh-ta parra*

**Can you take these if you are pregnant/breastfeeding?**
¿Se puede tomar esto estando embarazada/dando el pecho?
*seh pwehde tohmar estoh estandoh embarrathahda/dahndo el peh-tchoh*

**I normally take …**
Normalmente tomo …
*normalmenteh toh-moh*

**I'm allergic to …**
Soy alérgico a …
*soy allair-Heekoh a*

**Have you got anything for …?**
¿Tiene usted algo para …?
*tyeh-neh oosteh algoh parra*

**Do I need a prescription for …?**
¿Hace falta receta para …?
*ah-theh falta reh-theh-ta parra*

**I have lost a filling**
Se me ha caído un empaste
*seh meh a ka-_eedoh_ oon emp_a_steh*

**Will he/she be all right?**
¿Estará bien?
*estar_a_ byen*

**Will he/she need an operation?**
¿Va a necesitar una operación?
*ba a nethessee-t_a_r _oo_na oppeh-rath-y_o_n*

**How is she/he?**
¿Cómo está?
*k_oh_-moh est_a_*

---

## THINGS YOU'LL SEE

| | |
|---|---|
| **análisis clínicos** | clinical tests |
| **casa de socorro** | first-aid center |
| **clínica dental** | dentist's office |
| **consulta** | doctor's office |
| **farmacia de guardia** | pharmacy on duty |
| **ginecólogo** | gynecologist |
| **médico** | doctor |
| **médico general** | General Practitioner |
| **oculista** | optician |
| **otorrinolaringólogo** | ear, nose, and throat specialist |
| **pediatra** | pediatrician |
| **primeros auxilios** | first-aid center |
| **sala de espera** | waiting room |
| **test del embarazo** | pregnancy test |
| **tomamos la tensión** | take your blood pressure |
| **urgencias** | emergencies |

## THINGS YOU'LL HEAR

**Tome usted … comprimidos/pastillas cada vez**
Take … pills/tablets at a time

**Con agua**
With water

**Mastíquelos**
Chew them

**Una vez/dos veces/tres veces al día**
Once/twice/three times a day

**Al acostarse**
When you go to bed

**¿Qué toma normalmente?**
What do you normally take?

**Debería consultar a un médico**
I think you should see a doctor

**Lo siento, no lo tenemos**
I'm sorry, we don't have that

**Hace falta una receta médica para eso**
You need a prescription for that

# CONVERSION TABLES

## DISTANCES

A mile is 1.6km. To convert kilometers to miles, divide the km by 8 and multiply by 5. Convert miles to km by dividing the miles by 5 and multiplying by 8.

| miles | 0.62 | 1.24 | 1.86 | 2.43 | 3.11 | 3.73 | 4.35 | 6.21 |
|---|---|---|---|---|---|---|---|---|
| **miles** *or* km | 1 | 2 | 3 | 4 | 5 | 6 | 7 | 10 |
| km | 1.61 | 3.22 | 4.83 | 6.44 | 8.05 | 9.66 | 11.27 | 16.10 |

## WEIGHTS

The kilogram is equivalent to 2lb 3oz. To convert kg to lbs, divide by 5 and multiply by 11. One ounce is about 28 grams, and 8 oz about 227 grams; 1lb is therefore about 454 grams.

| lbs | 2.20 | 4.41 | 6.61 | 8.82 | 11.02 | 13.23 | 19.84 | 22.04 |
|---|---|---|---|---|---|---|---|---|
| **lbs** *or* kg | 1 | 2 | 3 | 4 | 5 | 6 | 9 | 10 |
| kg | 0.45 | 0.91 | 1.36 | 1.81 | 2.27 | 2.72 | 4.08 | 4.53 |

## TEMPERATURE

To convert degrees Celsius into Fahrenheit, the accurate method is to multiply the C° figure by 1.8 and add 32. Similarly, to convert F° to C°, subtract 32 from the F° figure and divide by 1.8.

| C° | -10 | 0 | 5 | 10 | 20 | 30 | 36.9 | 40 | 100 |
|---|---|---|---|---|---|---|---|---|---|
| F° | 14 | 32 | 41 | 50 | 68 | 86 | 98.4 | 104 | 212 |

## LIQUIDS

A liter is about 2.11 pints; a gallon is roughly 3.8 liters.

| gals | 0.27 | 0.53 | 1.33 | 2.65 | 5.31 | 7.96 | 13.26 |
|---|---|---|---|---|---|---|---|
| **gals** *or* liters | 1 | 2 | 5 | 10 | 20 | 30 | 50 |
| liters | 3.77 | 7.54 | 18.85 | 37.70 | 75.40 | 113.10 | 188.50 |

## TIRE PRESSURES

| lb/sq in | 18 | 20 | 22 | 24 | 26 | 28 | 30 | 33 |
|---|---|---|---|---|---|---|---|---|
| kg/sq cm | 1.3 | 1.4 | 1.5 | 1.7 | 1.8 | 2.0 | 2.1 | 2.3 |

# MINI-DICTIONARY

Where two forms of nouns or pronouns are given in the Spanish, the first is masculine and the second feminine; e.g. "they" **ellos/ellas**, "this one" **éste/ésta**.

There are two verbs "to be" in Spanish: **ser** is used to describe a permanent condition, such as nationality and occupation, and **estar** is used to describe a temporary condition. Both forms are given in this order in the dictionary.

**a** un/una *(see p 5)*
**about: about 16** alrededor de dieciséis
**accelerator** el acelerador
**accident** el accidente
**accommodations** el alojamiento
**ache** el dolor
**adaptor** el adaptador
**address** la dirección
**adhesive** el pegamento
**admission charge** el precio de entrada
**after** ... después de ...
**aftershave** el after-shave
**again** otra vez
**against** contra
**agency** la agencia
**AIDS** el Sida
**air** el aire
**air conditioning** el aire acondicionado
**aircraft** el avión
**airline** la compañía aérea
**airport** el aeropuerto
**airport bus** el autobús del aeropuerto
**aisle** el pasillo
**alarm clock** el despertador
**alcohol** el alcohol
**Algeria** Argelia
**all** todo
    **all the streets** todas las calles
    **that's all** eso es todo
**almost** casi

**alone** solo
**already** ya
**always** siempre
**am: I am** soy/estoy
**ambulance** la ambulancia
**America** América
**American** *(man)* el americano
    *(woman)* la americana
    *(adj.)* americano
**and** y; *(before word beginning with "i"*
    *or "hi")* e
**ankle** el tobillo
**another** otro
**answering machine** el contestador
    automático
**antifreeze** el anticongelante
**antiseptic** el antiséptico
**apartment** el apartamento, el piso
**aperitif** el aperitivo
**appetite** el apetito
**apple** la manzana
**application form** el impreso de solicitud
**appointment** *(business)* la cita
    *(at hair salon)* hora
**apricot** el albaricoque
**are: you are** es/está
    *(familiar)* eres/estás
    **we are** somos/estamos
    **they are** son/están
**arm** el brazo

**arrive** llegar
**art** el arte
**art gallery** la galería de arte
**artist** el/la artista
**as: as soon as possible** lo antes posible
**ashtray** el cenicero
**asleep: he's asleep** está dormido
**aspirin** la aspirina
**at: at the post office** en Correos
  **at night** por la noche
  **at 3 o'clock** a las tres
**ATM** el cajero automático
**ATM card** la tarjeta de banco
**Atlantic Ocean** el Océano Atlántico
**attractive** *(person)* guapo
  *(object)* bonito
  *(offer)* atractivo
**aunt** la tía
**Australia** Australia
**Australian** *(man)* el australiano
  *(woman)* la australiana
  *(adj.)* australiano
**auto-body shop** el taller
**automatic** automático
**away: is it far away?** ¿está lejos?
  **go away!** ¡váyase!
**awful** horrible
**ax** el hacha
**axle** el eje

**baby** el niño pequeño, el bebé
**baby carriage** el cochecito
**baby wipes** las toallitas para bebé
**back** *(not front)* la parte de atrás
  *(body)* la espalda
  **to come back** volver
**backpack** la mochila
**bacon** el bacon
  **bacon and eggs** huevos fritos
  con bacon
**bad** malo
**bag** la bolsa
**bait** el cebo
**bake** cocer al horno

**bakery** la panadería
**balcony** el balcón
**Balearic Islands** las (Islas) Baleares
**ball** la pelota
**ballpoint pen** el bolígrafo
**banana** el plátano
**band** *(musicians)* la banda
**bandage** la venda
**bangs** *(hair)* el flequillo
**bank** el banco
**bar** *(drinks)* el bar
  **bar of chocolate** una tableta de
  chocolate
**barbecue** la barbacoa
**barber's** la peluquería de caballeros
**bargain** la ganga
**basement** el sótano
**basin** *(sink)* el lavabo
**basket** el cesto
**bath** el baño
  **to take a bath** darse un baño
**bathing suit** el bañador,
  el traje de baño
**bathroom** el cuarto de baño
**battery** *(car)* la batería
  *(flashlight, etc.)* la pila
**Bay of Biscay** el Golfo de Vizcaya
**beach** la playa
**beach ball** el balón de playa
**beans** las judías
**beard** la barba
**beautiful** *(object)* precioso
  *(person)* guapo
**because** porque
**bed** la cama
**bed linen** la ropa de cama
**bedroom** el dormitorio
**beef** la carne de vaca
**beer** la cerveza
**before ...** antes de ...
**beginner** un/una principiante
**behind ...** detrás de ...
**beige** beige
**bell** *(church)* la campana
  *(door)* el timbre

**below** ... debajo de ...
**belt** el cinturón
**beside** al lado de
**best** (el) mejor
**better** mejor
**between** ... entre ...
**bicycle** la bicicleta
**big** grande
**bill** la cuenta
  *(money)* el billete de banco
**bird** el pájaro
**birthday** el cumpleaños
  **happy birthday!** ¡felicidades!
**birthday present**
  el regalo de cumpleaños
**bite** *(noun: by dog)* la mordedura
  *(by insect)* la picadura
  *(verb: by dog)* morder
  *(by insect)* picar
**bitter** amargo
**black** negro
**blackberries** las moras
**blackcurrants** las grosellas negras
**blanket** la manta
**bleach** *(noun)* la lejía
  *(verb: hair)* teñir
**blind** *(cannot see)* ciego
**blinds** las persianas
**blister** una ampolla
**blizzard** la ventisca
**blond(e)** *(adj.)* rubio
**blood** la sangre
**blouse** la blusa
**blue** azul
**boat** el barco
  *(small)* la barca
**body** el cuerpo
**boil** *(of water)* hervir
  *(egg, etc.)* cocer
**bolt** *(noun: on door)* el cerrojo
  *(verb)* echar el cerrojo
**bone** el hueso
**book** *(noun)* el libro
  *(verb)* reservar
**bookstore** la librería

**boot** la bota
**border** el borde
  *(between countries)* la frontera
**boring** aburrido
**born: I was born in** ...
  nací en ...
**both: both of them** los dos
  **both of us** los dos
  **both ... and ...**
  tanto ... como ...
**bottle** la botella
**bottle opener** el abrebotellas
**bottom** el fondo
  *(part of body)* el trasero
**bowl** el cuenco
**box** la caja
**box office** la taquilla
**boy** el chico
**boyfriend** el novio
**bra** el sostén
**bracelet** la pulsera
**braces** los tirantes
**brake** *(noun)* el freno
  *(verb)* frenar
**brandy** el coñac
**bread** el pan
**breakdown** *(car)* la avería
  *(nervous)* la crisis nerviosa
  **I've had a breakdown** *(car)*
  he tenido una avería
**breakfast** el desayuno
**breathe** respirar
**bridge** el puente
  *(game)* el bridge
**briefcase** la cartera
**British** británico
**brochure** el folleto
**broiler** la parrilla
**broken** roto
**brooch** el broche
**brother** el hermano
**brown** marrón
  *(hair)* castaño
  *(skin)* moreno
**bruise** el cardenal

**brush** (*noun: hair*) el cepillo del pelo
  (*paint*) la brocha
  (*for cleaning*) el cepillo
  (*verb: hair*) cepillar el pelo
**bucket** el cubo
**building** el edificio
**bull** el toro
**bullfight** la corrida de toros
**bullfighter** el torero
**bullring** la plaza de toros
**bumper** el parachoques
**burglar** el ladrón
**burn** (*noun*) la quemadura
  (*verb*) quemar
**bus** el autobús
  (*long-distance*) el autobús
**business** el negocio
  **it's none of your business** no es
  asunto suyo
**bus station** la estación de autobuses
**busy** (*occupied*) ocupado
  (*bar*) concurrido
**but** pero
**butcher's** la carnicería
**butter** la mantequilla
**button** el botón
**buy** comprar
**by: by the window** junto a la ventana
  **by Friday** para el viernes
  **by myself** yo solo
  **written by …** escrito por …

**cabbage** la col
**cabinet** el armario
**cable car** el teleférico
**cable TV** la televisión por cable
**café** el café
**cake** (*small*) el pastel
  (*large*) la tarta
  **sponge cake** el bizcocho
**calculator** la calculadora
**call: what's it called?** ¿cómo se llama?
**camcorder** la videocámara
**camera** la máquina de fotos

**campsite** el camping
**camshaft** el árbol de levas
**can: can you …?** ¿puede …?
  **I can't …** no puedo …
**can** (*tin*) la lata
**Canada** Canadá
**Canadian** el/la canadiense
  (*adj.*) canadiense
**canal** el canal
**Canaries** las (Islas) Canarias
**candle** la vela
**candy** el caramelo
**can opener** el abrelatas
**cap** (*bottle*) el tapón
  (*hat*) la gorra
**car** el coche
  (*train*) el vagón
**carbonated** con gas
**carburetor** el carburador
**card** la tarjeta
**cardigan** la rebeca
**careful** prudente
  **be careful!** ¡cuidado!
**caretaker** el portero, el encargado
**carpet** la alfombra
**carrot** la zanahoria
**car seat** (*for a baby/child*) el asiento
  infantil
**case** (*suitcase*) la maleta
**cash** (*noun*) el dinero
  (*verb*) cobrar
  **to pay cash** pagar al contado
**cassette** la cassette, la cinta
**cassette player** el cassette
**castanets** unas castañuelas
**Castile** Castilla
**Castilian** castellano
**castle** el castillo
**cat** el gato
**Catalonia** Cataluña
**cathedral** la catedral
**Catholic** (*adj.*) católico
**cauliflower** la coliflor
**cave** la cueva
**cemetery** el cementerio

**center** el centro
**central heating** la calefacción central
**certificate** el certificado
**chair** la silla
**change** *(noun: money)* el cambio
  *(verb: money)* cambiar
  *(clothes)* cambiarse
  *(trains, etc.)* hacer transbordo
**check** *(noun)* el cheque
**checkbook** el talonario de cheques
**check-in** *(desk)* (el mostrador de) facturación
**check in** *(verb)* facturar
**cheers!** *(toast)* ¡salud!
**cheese** el queso
**cherry** la cereza
**chess** el ajedrez
**chest** *(part of body)* el pecho
  *(furniture)* el arcón
**chest of drawers** la cómoda
**chewing gum** el chicle
**chicken** el pollo
**child** el niño
  *(female)* la niña
**children** los niños
**china** la porcelana
**chocolate** el chocolate
  **box of chocolates** una caja de bombones
**chop** *(food)* la chuleta
  *(verb: cut)* cortar
**church** la iglesia
**cigar** el puro
**cigarette** el cigarrillo
**cinema** el cine
**city** la ciudad
**city center** el centro (urbano)
**class** la clase
**classical music** la música clásica
**clean** *(adj.)* limpio
**clear** *(obvious)* evidente
  *(water)* claro
**clever** listo
**clock** el reloj

**close** *(near)* cerca
  *(stuffy)* sofocante
  *(verb)* cerrar
**closed** cerrado
**clothes** la ropa
**clubs** *(cards)* tréboles
**coat** el abrigo
**coat hanger** la percha
**cockroach** la cucaracha
**coffee** el café
**coin** la moneda
**cold** *(illness)* un resfriado
  *(adj.)* frío
  **I have a cold** tengo un resfriado
  **I am cold** tengo frío
**collar** el cuello
  *(of animal)* el collar
**collection** *(stamps, etc.)* la colección
  *(postal)* la recogida
**color** el color
**color film** la película en color
**comb** *(noun)* el peine
  *(verb)* peinar
**come** venir
  **I come from ...** soy de ...
  **we came last week** llegamos la semana pasada
  **come here!** ¡venga aquí!
**comforter** el edredón
**compact disk** el disco compacto
**compartment** el compartimento
**complicated** complicado
**computer** el ordenador
**concert** el concierto
**conditioner** *(hair)* el acondicionador
**condom** el condón
**conductor** *(bus)* el cobrador
  *(orchestra)* el director
**congratulations!** ¡enhorabuena!
**consulate** el consulado
**contact lenses** las lentes de contacto
**contraceptive** el anticonceptivo
**cook** *(noun)* el cocinero
  *(female)* la cocinera
  *(verb)* guisar

**cookie** la galleta
**cooking utensils** los utensilios de cocina
**cool** fresco
**cork** el corcho
**corkscrew** el sacacorchos
**corner** *(of street)* la esquina
  *(of room)* el rincón
**corridor** el pasillo
**cosmetics** los cosméticos
**cost** *(verb)* costar
  **what does it cost?** ¿cuánto cuesta?
**cotton** el algodón
**cotton balls** el algodón
**cough** *(noun)* la tos
  *(verb)* toser
**cough drops** las pastillas para la garganta
**country** *(state)* el país
  *(not town)* el campo
**cousin** el primo
  *(female)* la prima
**crab** el cangrejo
**cramp** el calambre
**crayfish** las cigalas
**cream** *(dairy)* la nata
  *(lotion)* la crema
**credit card** la tarjeta de crédito
**crib** el capazo
**crowded** lleno
**cruise** el crucero
**crutches** las muletas
**cry** *(weep)* llorar
  *(shout)* gritar
**cucumber** el pepino
**cuff links** los gemelos
**cup** la taza
**curlers** los rulos
**curls** los rizos
**curry** el curry
**curtain** la cortina
**customs** la aduana
**cut** *(noun)* la cortadura
  *(verb)* cortar

**dad** papá
**damp** húmedo
**dance** *(noun)* el baile
  *(verb)* bailar
**dangerous** peligroso
**dark** oscuro
  **dark blue** azul oscuro
**daughter** la hija
**day** el día
**dead** muerto
**deaf** sordo
**dear** *(person)* querido
**deck of cards** la baraja
**deep** profundo
**delayed** retrasado
**deliberately** a propósito
**dentist** el/la dentista
**dentures** la dentadura postiza
**deny** negar
**deodorant** el desodorante
**department store** los grandes almacenes
**departure** la salida
**departure lounge** salidas
**develop** *(film)* revelar
**diamonds** *(jewels)* los diamantes
  *(cards)* diamantes
**diaper** el pañal
**diarrhea** la diarrea
**diary** la agenda
**dictionary** el diccionario
**die** morir
**diesel** *(oil)* fuel-oil
  *(adj.: engine)* diesel
**different** diferente
  **that's different!** ¡eso es distinto!
  **I'd like a different one** quería otro distinto
**difficult** difícil
**dining room** el comedor
**dirty** sucio
**disabled** minusválido
**dish cloth** el paño de cocina
**dishwashing detergent** el lavavajillas
**disposable diapers** pañales desechables
**distributor** *(car)* el distribuidor

**divorced** divorciado
**do** hacer
  **how do you do?** ¿qué tal?
**dock** el muelle
**doctor** el médico
  *(female)* la médica
**document** el documento
**dog** el perro
**doll** la muñeca
**dollar** el dólar
**door** la puerta
**double room** la habitación doble
**doughnut** el dónut®
**down** hacia abajo
**dress** el vestido
**drink** *(noun)* la bebida
  *(verb)* beber
  **would you like a drink?** ¿quiere beber algo?
**drinking water** agua potable
**drive** *(verb)* conducir
**driver** el conductor
**driving regulations** el código de la circulación
**driver's license** el carnet de conducir
**drunk** borracho
**dry** seco
  *(sherry)* fino
**during** durante
**dust cloth** el trapo del polvo
**duty-free** libre de impuestos
  **duty-free shop** el duty-free

**each** *(every)* cada
  **20 euros each** viente euros cada uno
**ear** *(inner)* el oído
  *(outer)* la oreja
  **ears** las orejas
**early** temprano
**earrings** los pendientes
**east** el Este
**easy** fácil
**eat** comer

**egg** el huevo
**either: either of them** cualquiera de ellos
  **either … or …** o bien … o …
**elastic** elástico
**elbow** el codo
**electric** eléctrico
**electricity** la electricidad
**elevator** el ascensor
**else: something else** algo más
  **someone else** alguien más
  **somewhere else** en otro sitio
**email** el email
**email address** la dirección de email
**embarrassing** embarazoso
**embassy** la embajada
**embroidery** el bordado
**emergency** la emergencia
**emergency brake** *(train)* el freno de emergencia
**emergency exit** la salida de emergencia
**empty** vacío
**end** el final
**engaged** *(couple)* prometido
**engine** *(motor)* el motor
**England** Inglaterra
**English** inglés
**Englishman** el inglés
**Englishwoman** la inglesa
**enlargement** la ampliación
**enough** bastante
**entertainment** las diversiones
**entrance** la entrada
**envelope** el sobre
**eraser** la goma de borrar
**escalator** la escalera mecánica
**especially** sobre todo
**evening** la tarde
**every** cada
  **every day** todos los días
**everyone** todos
**everything** todo
**everywhere** por todas partes
**example** el ejemplo
  **for example** por ejemplo
**excellent** excelente

**excess baggage** exceso de equipaje
**exchange** *(verb)* cambiar
**exchange rate** el cambio
**excursion** la excursión
**excuse me!** *(to get attention)* ¡oiga,
  por favor!
  *(when sneezing, etc.)* ¡perdón!
  **excuse me, please** *(to get past)*
  ¿me hace el favor?
**exit** la salida
**expensive** caro
**extension cord** el cable alargador
**eye** el ojo

**face** la cara
**faint** *(unclear)* tenue
  *(verb)* desmayarse
**fair** *(noun)* la feria
  **it's not fair** no hay derecho
**false teeth** la dentadura postiza
**family** la familia
**fan** *(ventilator)* el ventilador
  *(handheld)* el abanico
  *(enthusiast)* el fan
  *(football)* el hincha
**fantastic** fantástico
**far** lejos
  **how far is it to …?**
  ¿qué distancia hay a …?
**fare** el billete
**farm** la granja
**farmer** el granjero
**fashion** la moda
**fast** rápido
**fat** *(person)* gordo
  *(on meat, etc.)* la grasa
**father** el padre
**faucet** el grifo
**fax** *(noun)* el fax
  *(verb: document)* enviar por fax
**feel** *(touch)* tocar
  **I feel hot** tengo calor
  **I feel like …** me apetece …
  **I don't feel well** no me encuentro bien

**felt-tip pen** el rotulador
**fence** la cerca
**ferry** el ferry
**fiancé** el prometido
**fiancée** la prometida
**field** el campo
**fig** el higo
**filling** *(in tooth)* el empaste
  *(in sandwich, cake)* el relleno
**film** la película
**filter** el filtro
**filter papers** los papeles de filtro
**finger** el dedo
**fire** el fuego
  *(blaze)* el incendio
**fire extinguisher** el extintor
**fireworks** los fuegos artificiales
**first** primero
  **first aid** primeros auxilios
**first name** el nombre de pila
**fish** el pez
  *(food)* el pescado
**fishing** la pesca
  **to go fishing** ir a pescar
**fish market** la pescadería
**flag** la bandera
**flash** *(camera)* el flash
**flashlight** la linterna
**flat** *(level)* plano
**flavor** el sabor
**flea** la pulga
**flight** el vuelo
**floor** el suelo
  *(story)* el piso
**flour** la harina
**flower** la flor
**flute** la flauta
**fly** *(insect)* la mosca
  *(verb: of plane, insect)* volar
  *(of person)* viajar en avión
**fog** la niebla
**folk music** la música folklórica
**food** la comida
**food poisoning** la intoxicación
  alimenticia

**foot** el pie
**for: for me** para mí
  **what for?** ¿para qué?
  **for a week** (para) una semana
**foreigner** el extranjero
  (*female*) la extranjera
**forest** el bosque
  (*tropical*) la selva
**forget** olvidar
**fork** el tenedor
**fountain pen** la (pluma) estilográfica
**fourth** cuarto
**France** Francia
**free** (*not engaged*) libre
  (*no charge*) gratis
**freezer** el congelador
**French** francés
**french fries** las patatas fritas
**friend** el amigo
  (*female*) la amiga
**friendly** simpático
**front: in front of …** delante de …
**frost** la escarcha
**fruit** la fruta
**fruit juice** el zumo de frutas
**fry** freír
**frying pan** la sartén
**full** lleno
  **I'm full** (*up*) estoy lleno
**full board** pensión completa
**funny** divertido
  (*odd*) raro
**furniture** los muebles

**garage** (*for parking*) el garage
**garbage** la basura
**garbage can** el cubo de la basura
**garbage can liner** la bolsa de basura
**garden** el jardín
**garlic** el ajo
**gas** la gasolina
**gas station** la gasolinera
**gas-permeable lenses** las lentes de
  contacto semi-rígidas

**gate** la puerta
  (*at airport*) la puerta de embarque
**gay** (*homosexual*) gay
**gear shift** la palanca de velocidades
**gel** (*hair*) el gel
**German** alemán
**Germany** Alemania
**get** (*fetch*) traer
  **have you got …?** ¿tiene …?
  **to get the train** coger el tren
**get back: we get back tomorrow** nos
  volvemos mañana
  **to get something back** recobrar algo
**get in** (*of train, etc.*) subirse
  (*of person*) llegar
**get off** (*bus, etc.*) bajarse
**get on** (*bus, etc.*) subirse
**get out** bajarse
  (*bring out*) sacar
**get up** (*rise*) levantarse
**Gibraltar** Gibraltar
**gift** el regalo
**gin** la ginebra
**ginger** (*spice*) el jengibre
**girl** la chica
**girlfriend** la novia
**give** dar
**glad** alegre
**glass** (*material*) el cristal
  (*for drinking*) el vaso
**glasses** las gafas
**glossy prints** las copias con brillo
**gloves** los guantes
**glue** el pegamento
**go** ir
**gold** el oro
**good** bueno
  **good!** ¡bien!
**goodbye** adiós
**government** el gobierno
**granddaughter** la nieta
**grandfather** el abuelo
**grandmother** la abuela
**grandparents** los abuelos
**grandson** el nieto

**grapes** las uvas
**grass** la hierba
**gray** gris
**Great Britain** Gran Bretaña
**green** verde
**grocer's** la tienda de comestibles
**groundcloth** la lona impermeable
**ground floor** la planta baja
**guarantee** *(noun)* la garantía
  *(verb)* garantizar
**guide** el/la guía
**guide book** la guía turística
**guitar** la guitarra
**gun** *(rifle)* la escopeta
  *(pistol)* la pistola

**hair** el pelo
**haircut** el corte de pelo
**hair dryer** el secador (de pelo)
**hair salon** la peluquería
**hairspray** la laca
**half** medio
  **half an hour** media hora
**half board** media pensión
**ham** el jamón
**hamburger** la hamburguesa
**hammer** el martillo
**hand** la mano
**handbrake** el freno de mano
**handle** *(door)* el picaporte
**handsome** guapo
**hangover** la resaca
**happy** contento
**harbor** el puerto
**hard** duro
  *(difficult)* difícil
**hardware store** la ferretería
**hat** el sombrero
  *(woollen)* el gorro
**have** tener
  **I don't have …** no tengo …
  **do you have …?** ¿tiene …?
  **I have to go** tengo que irme
  **can I have …?** ¿me da …?

**hay fever** la fiebre del heno
**he** él
**head** la cabeza
**headache** el dolor de cabeza
**hear** oír
**hearing aid** el audífono
**heart** el corazón
**hearts** *(cards)* corazones
**heater** la estufa
**heating** la calefacción
**heavy** pesado
**heel** el talón
  *(shoe)* el tacón
**hello** hola
  *(on phone)* dígame
**help** *(noun)* la ayuda
  *(verb)* ayudar
**hepatitis** la hepatitis
**her: it's for her** es para ella
  **give it to her** déselo
  **her book** su libro
  **her shoes** sus zapatos
  **it's hers** es suyo
**high** alto
**highway** la autopista
**hill** el monte
**him: it's for him** es para él
  **give it to him** déselo
**hire** alquilar
**his: his book** su libro
  **his shoes** sus zapatos
  **it's his** es suyo
**history** la historia
**hitchhike** hacer auto-stop
**HIV positive** seropositivo
**hobby** el hobby
**home: at home** en casa
**homeopathy** la homeopatía
**honest** honrado
  *(sincere)* sincero
**honey** la miel
**honeymoon** el viaje de novios
**hood** *(car)* el capó
**horn** *(car)* el claxon
  *(animal)* el cuerno

**horrible** horrible
**hospital** el hospital
**hour** la hora
**house** la casa
**hovercraft** el aerodeslizador
**how?** ¿cómo?
**hungry: I'm hungry** tengo hambre
**hurry: I'm in a hurry** tengo prisa
**husband** el marido
**hydrofoil** la hidroaleta

**I** yo
**ice** el hielo
**ice cream** el helado
**ice skates** los patines para hielo
**if** si
**ignition** el encendido
**immediately** inmediatamente
**impossible** imposible
**in** en
    **in English** en inglés
    **in the hotel** en el hotel
    **in Barcelona** en Barcelona
    **he's not in** no está
**inexpensive** barato
**infection** la infección
**information** la información
**inhaler** (for asthma, etc.) el spray,
    el inhalador
**injection** la inyección
**injury** la herida
**ink** la tinta
**inn** la fonda
**inner tube** la cámara (neumática)
**insect** el insecto
**insect repellent** la loción anti-mosquitos
**insomnia** el insomnio
**instant coffee** el café instantáneo
**insurance** el seguro
**interesting** interesante
**internet** el internet
**interpret** interpretar
**interpreter** el/la intérprete
**invitation** la invitación

**Ireland** Irlanda
**Irish** irlandés
**Irishman** el irlandés
**Irishwoman** la irlandesa
**iron** (material) el hierro
    (for clothes) la plancha
    (verb) planchar
**is** es/está
**island** la isla
**it** lo/la
**Italian** (adj.) italiano
**Italy** Italia
**its** su

**jacket** la chaqueta
**jam** la mermelada
**jazz** el jazz
**jeans** los tejanos, los vaqueros
**jellyfish** la medusa
**jeweler's** la joyería
**job** el trabajo
**jog** (verb) hacer footing
**jogging suit** el chandal
**joke** la broma
    (story) el chiste
**just** (only) sólo
    **it's just arrived**
    acaba de llegar

**kettle** el hervidor de agua
**key** la llave
**kidney** el riñón
**kilo** el kilo
**kilometer** el kilómetro
**kitchen** la cocina
**knee** la rodilla
**knife** el cuchillo
**knit** hacer punto
**knitwear** artículos de punto
**know** saber
    (person, place) conocer
    **I don't know** no sé

label la etiqueta
lace el encaje
laces (shoe) los cordones (de los zapatos)
lady la señora
lake el lago
lamb el cordero
lamp la lámpara
lampshade la pantalla
land (noun) la tierra
  (verb) aterrizar
language el idioma
large grande
last (final) último
  last week la semana pasada
  at last! ¡por fin!
late: it's getting late se está haciendo tarde
  the bus is late el autobús se ha retrasado
later más tarde
laugh reír
Laundromat la lavandería automática
laundry (dirty) la ropa sucia
  (washed) la colada
laundry detergent el detergente
laxative el laxante
lazy perezoso
leaf la hoja
leaflet el folleto
learn aprender
leather el cuero
left (not right) izquierdo
  there's nothing left no queda nada
leg la pierna
lemon el limón
lemonade la limonada
length la longitud
lens la lente
less menos
lesson la clase
letter (mail) la carta
  (of alphabet) la letra
letter carrier el cartero
lettuce la lechuga
library la biblioteca
license el permiso

license plate la matrícula
life la vida
light (noun) la luz
  (adj.. not heavy) ligero
  (not dark) claro
light bulb la bombilla
lighter el encendedor
lighter fuel el gas para el encendedor
light meter el fotómetro
like: I like it me gusta
  I like swimming me gusta nadar
  it's like … es como …
  like this one como éste
lime (fruit) la lima
line (noun) la cola
  (verb) hacer cola
lipstick la barra de labios
liqueur el licor
list la lista
liter el litro
litter la basura
little (small) pequeño
  it's a little big es un poco grande
  just a little sólo un poquito
liver el hígado
lobster la langosta
lollipop el chupa-chups
long largo
lost and found office la oficina de objetos perdidos
lot: a lot mucho
loud alto
lounge (in house) el cuarto de estar
  (in hotel, etc.) el salón
lounge chair la tumbona
love (noun) el amor
  (verb) querer
  I love Spain me encanta España
lover el/la amante
low bajo
luck la suerte
  good luck! ¡suerte!
luggage el equipaje
luggage rack la rejilla de equipajes
lunch la comida

mad loco
magazine la revista
mail el correo
mailbox el buzón
Majorca Mallorca
make hacer
make-up el maquillaje
man el hombre
manager el/la gerente
  (hotel: male) el director
  (female) la directora
many: not many no muchos
map el mapa
  a map of Madrid un plano de Madrid
marble el mármol
margarine la margarina
market el mercado
marmalade la mermelada de naranja
married casado
mascara el rímel
mass (church) la misa
match (light) la cerilla
  (sport) el partido
material (cloth) la tela
matter: it doesn't matter no importa
mattress el colchón
maybe quizás
me: it's for me es para mí
  give it to me démelo
meal la comida
mean: what does this mean?
  ¿qué significa esto?
meat la carne
mechanic el mecánico
medicine la medicina
Mediterranean el Mediterráneo
medium (sherry) amontillado
medium-dry (wine) semi-seco
meeting la reunión
melon el melón
menu la carta
  fixed-price menu el menú (del día)
message el recado
middle: in the middle en el centro
midnight medianoche

milk la leche
mine: it's mine es mío
mineral water el agua mineral
minute el minuto
mirror el espejo
Miss Señorita
mistake la equivocación
mobile phone el teléfono móvil
modem el modem
mom mamá
money el dinero
month el mes
monument el monumento
moon la luna
moped el ciclomotor
more más
morning la mañana
  in the morning por la mañana
Morocco Marruecos
mosaic el mosaico
mosquito el mosquito
mother la madre
motorboat la motora
motorcycle la motocicleta
mountain la montaña
mountain bike la bicicleta de montaña
mouse el ratón
mousse (for hair) espuma moldeadora
mouth la boca
move (verb: something) mover
  (oneself) moverse
  (house) mudarse (de casa)
  don't move! ¡no se mueva!
movie la película
Mr. Señor
Mrs. Señora
much: much better mucho mejor
  much slower mucho más despacio
mug la jarrita
museum el museo
mushroom la seta
music la música
musical instrument el instrumento
  musical
musician el músico

**mussels** los mejillones
**must: I must …** tengo que …
**mustache** el bigote
**mustard** la mostaza
**my: my book** mi libro
  **my keys** mis llaves

**nail** *(metal)* el clavo
  *(finger)* la uña
**nail clippers** los cortauñas
**nailfile** la lima de uñas
**nail polish** el esmalte de uñas
**name** el nombre
  **what's your name?** ¿cómo se llama
  usted?
**napkin** la servilleta
**narrow** estrecho
**near: near the door** junto a la puerta
  **near New York** cerca de New York
**necessary** necesario
**neck** el cuello
**necklace** el collar
**need** *(verb)* necesitar
  **I need …** necesito …
  **there's no need** no hace falta
**needle** la aguja
**negative** *(photo)* el negativo
**neither: neither of them**
  ninguno de ellos
  **neither … nor …** ni … ni …
**nephew** el sobrino
**never** nunca
**new** nuevo
**news** las noticias
**newspaper** el periódico
**newsstand** el kiosko de periódicos
**New Zealand** Nueva Zelanda
**New Zealander**
  *(man)* el neozelandés
  *(woman)* la neozelandesa
  *(adj.)* neozelandés
**next** siguiente
  **next week** la semana que viene
  **what next?** ¿y ahora qué?

**nice** bonito
  *(pleasant)* agradable
  *(to eat)* bueno
**niece** la sobrina
**night** la noche
**nightclub** la discoteca
**nightgown** el camisón
**night porter** el vigilante nocturno
**no** *(response)* no
  **I have no money** no tengo dinero
**nobody** nadie
**noisy** ruidoso
**noon** mediodía
**north** el norte
**Northern Ireland** Irlanda del Norte
**nose** la nariz
**not** no
  **he's not …** no es/está …
**notebook** el cuaderno
**nothing** nada
**novel** la novela
**now** ahora
**nowhere** en ninguna parte
**nudist** el/la nudista
**number** el número
**nut** *(fruit)* la nuez
  *(for bolt)* la tuerca

**oars** los remos
**occasionally** de vez en cuando
**occupied** ocupado
**octopus** el pulpo
**of** de
**office** *(place)* la oficina
  *(room)* el despacho
**often** a menudo
**oil** el aceite
**ointment** la pomada
**OK** vale
**old** viejo
  **how old are you?** ¿cuántos años tiene?
**olive** la aceituna
**olive oil** el aceite de oliva
**olive tree** el olivo

omelette la tortilla
on … en …
one uno
onion la cebolla
only sólo
open (adj.) abierto
  (verb) abrir
operation la operación
operator la operadora
opposite: opposite the hotel enfrente
  del hotel
optician el oculista
or o
orange (fruit) la naranja
  (color) naranja
orange juice el zumo de naranja
orchestra la orquesta
ordinary corriente
organ (music) el órgano
other: the other (one) el otro
our nuestro
  it's ours es nuestro
out: he's out no está
outside fuera
oven el horno
over … encima de …
  (more than) más de …
  it's over the road está al otro lado
  de la calle
  when the party is over
  cuando termine la fiesta
  over there allí
oyster la ostra

package (parcel) el paquete
packet el paquete
  (cigarettes) la cajetilla
  (candy, chips) la bolsa
padlock el candado
page la página
pain el dolor
paint (noun) la pintura
pair el par
pajamas el pijama

palace el palacio
pale pálido
pancakes las crepes
pants los pantalones
pantyhose los pantis
paper el papel
  (newspaper) el periódico
paraffin la parafina
parcel el paquete
pardon? ¿cómo dice?
parents los padres
park (noun) el parque
  (verb) aparcar
parking lights las luces de posición
parsley el perejil
part (hair) la raya
party (celebration) la fiesta
  (group) el grupo
  (political) el partido
pass (in car) adelantar
passenger el pasajero
passport el pasaporte
pasta la pasta
path el camino
pay pagar
peach el melocotón
peanuts los cacahuetes
pear la pera
pearl la perla
peas los guisantes
pedestrian el peatón
pen la pluma
pen pal el amigo por correspondencia
  (female) la amiga por correspondencia
pencil el lápiz
pencil sharpener el sacapuntas
people la gente
pepper la pimienta
  (red, green) el pimiento
peppermints las pastillas de menta
per: per night por noche
perfect perfecto
perfume el perfume
perhaps quizás
perm la permanente

**petticoat** la combinacíion
**pharmacy** la farmacia
**phone book** la guía telefónica
**phone booth** la cabina telefónica
**phonecard** la tarjeta telefónica
**photocopier** la fotocopiadora
**photograph** *(noun)* la foto(grafía)
  *(verb)* fotografiar
**photographer** el fotógrafo
**phrase book** el libro de frases
**piano** el piano
**pickpocket** el carterista
**picnic** el picnic
**piece** el pedazo
**pill** la pastilla
**pillow** la almohada
**pilot** el piloto
**pin** el alfiler
  *(clothes)* la pinza
**pine** *(tree)* el pino
**pineapple** la piña
**pink** rosa
**pipe** *(for smoking)* la pipa
  *(for water)* la tubería
**piston** el pistón
**pizza** la pizza
**place** el lugar
  **at your place** en su casa
**plant** la planta
**plastic** el plástico
**plastic bag** la bolsa de plástico
**plastic wrap** el plástico para envolver
**plate** el plato
**platform** el andén
**play** *(theater)* la obra de teatro
  *(verb)* jugar
**please** por favor
**plug** *(electrical)* el enchufe
  *(sink)* el tapón
**pocket** el bolsillo
**pocketbook** el bolso
**pocketknife** la navaja
**poison** el veneno
**police** la policía
**police officer** el policía

**police station** la comisaría
**politics** la política
**poor** pobre
  *(bad quality)* malo
**pop music** la música pop
**pork** la carne de cerdo
**port** *(harbor)* el puerto
  *(drink)* el oporto
**porter** *(hotel)* el conserje
**Portugal** Portugal
**Portuguese** portugués
**possible** posible
**post** *(noun)* el correo
  *(verb)* echar al correo
**postcard** la postal
**poster** el póster
**post office** (la oficina de) Correos
**potato** la patata
**potato chips** las patatas fritas
**poultry** las aves
**pound** *(money)* la libra
  *(weight)* la libra
**powder** el polvo
  *(make up)* los polvos
**prawns** las gambas
**prefer** preferir
**prescription** la receta
**pretty** bonito
  *(quite)* bastante
**priest** el cura
**private** privado
**problem** el problema
**protection factor (SPF)** el factor de
  protección
**public** público
**pull** tirar de
**puncture** el pinchazo
**purple** morado
**purse** el monedero
**push** empujar
**put** poner
**Pyrenees** los Pirineos

**quality** la calidad
**quarter** un cuarto
**question** la pregunta
**quick** rápido
**quiet** tranquilo
  *(person)* callado
**quite** *(fairly)* bastante
  *(fully)* completamente

**radiator** el radiador
**radio** la radio
**radish** el rábano
**railroad** el ferrocarril
**rain** la lluvia
**rain boots** las botas de agua
**raincoat** la gabardina
**raisins** las pasas
**raspberry** la frambuesa
**rare** *(uncommon)* raro
  *(steak)* poco pasado
**rat** la rata
**razor blades** las cuchillas de afeitar
**read** leer
**reading lamp** el flexo
  *(bedside)* la lamparilla de noche
**ready** listo
**receipt** el recibo
**receptionist** el/la recepcionista
**record** *(music)* el disco
  *(sport, etc.)* el récord
**record player** el tocadiscos
**record store** la tienda de discos
**red** rojo
  *(wine)* tinto
**refreshments** los refrescos
**refrigerator** el frigorífico
**relative** el pariente
**relax** relajarse
  *(rest)* descansar
**religion** la religión
**remember: I remember** me acuerdo
  **I don't remember** no me acuerdo
**rent** *(verb)* alquilar
**reservation** la reserva

**rest** *(noun: remainder)* el resto
  *(verb: relax)* descansar
**restaurant** el restaurante
**restaurant car** el vagón-restaurante
**restroom** *(men)* los servicios de caballeros
  *(women)* los servicios de señoras
**return** *(come back)* volver
  *(give back)* devolver
**return ticket** el billete de ida y vuelta
**rice** el arroz
**rich** rico
**right** *(correct)* correcto
  *(not left)* derecho
**ring** *(wedding, etc.)* el anillo
**ripe** maduro
**river** el río
**road** la carretera
**rock** *(stone)* la roca
  *(music)* el rock
**roll** *(bread)* el bollo
**roof** el tejado
**room** la habitación
  *(space)* sitio
**rope** la cuerda
**rose** la rosa
**round** *(circular)* redondo
  **it's my round** me toca a mí
**row** *(verb)* remar
**rowboat** la barca de remos
**rubber** *(material)* la goma
**rubber band** la goma
**ruby** *(stone)* el rubí
**rug** *(mat)* la alfombra
  *(blanket)* la manta
**ruins** las ruinas
**ruler** *(for drawing)* la regla
**rum** el ron
**run** *(verb)* correr
**runway** la pista

**sad** triste
**safe** *(not dangerous)* seguro
**safety pin** el imperdible

**sailboard** la tabla de windsurfing
**sailboat** el balandro
**salad** la ensalada
**sale** (*at reduced prices*) las rebajas
**salmon** el salmón
**salt** la sal
**same: the same dress** el mismo vestido
  **the same people** la misma gente
  **same again, please** lo mismo otra vez,
  por favor
**sand** la arena
**sandals** las sandalias
**sand dunes** las dunas
**sandwich** el bocadillo
**sanitary napkins** las compresas
**sauce** la salsa
**saucepan** el cazo
**sauna** la sauna
**sausage** la salchicha
**say** decir
  **what did you say?** ¿qué ha dicho?
  **how do you say ...?** ¿cómo se dice ...?
**scampi** las gambas
**scarf** la bufanda
  (*head*) el pañuelo
**school** la escuela
**scissors** las tijeras
**Scotland** Escocia
**Scotsman** el escocés
**Scotswoman** la escocesa
**Scottish** escocés
**screw** el tornillo
**screwdriver** el destornillador
**sea** el mar
**seafood** mariscos
**seat** el asiento
**seat belt** el cinturón de seguridad
**second** el segundo
**second floor** el primer piso
**see** ver
  **I can't see** no veo
  **I see** comprendo
**sell** vender
**separate** (*adj.*) distinto
**separated** separado

**serious** serio
**several** varios
**sew** coser
**shampoo** el champú
**shave** (*noun*) un afeitado
  **to have a shave** afeitarse
**shaving foam** la espuma de
  afeitar
**shawl** el chal
**she** ella
**sheet** la sábana
  (*of paper*) la hoja
**shell** la concha
**shellfish** mariscos
**sherry** el jerez
**ship** el barco
**shirt** la camisa
**shoelaces** los cordones de los zapatos
**shoe polish** la crema de zapatos
**shoes** los zapatos
**shop** la tienda
**shopping** la compra
  **to go shopping** ir de compras
**short** corto
**shorts** los pantalones cortos
**shoulder** el hombro
**shower** (*bath*) la ducha
  (*rain*) el chaparrón
**shower gel** el gel de ducha
**shrimp** las quisquillas
**shutter** (*camera*) el obturador
  (*window*) el postigo
**sick: I feel sick** tengo náuseas
  **to be sick** (*vomit*) devolver
**side** (*edge*) el borde
**sidewalk** la acera
**sights: the sights of ...** los lugares
  de interés de ...
**silk** la seda
**silver** (*metal*) la plata
  (*color*) plateado
**simple** sencillo
**sing** cantar
**single** (*one*) único
  (*unmarried*) soltero

single room la habitación individual
sister la hermana
skid patinar
skiing: to go skiing ir a esquiar
skin cleanser la leche limpiadora
ski resort la estación de esquí
skirt la falda
skis los esquís
sky el cielo
sleep (noun) el sueño
  (verb) dormir
sleeper el coche-cama
sleeping bag el saco de dormir
sleeping pill el somnífero
slippers las zapatillas
slow lento
small pequeño
smell (noun) el olor
  (verb) oler
smile (noun) la sonrisa
  (verb) sonreír
smoke (noun) el humo
  (verb) fumar
snack la comida ligera
sneakers los zapatos de deporte
snow la nieve
so: so good tan bueno
  not so much no tanto
soaking solution (for contact lenses)
  la solución limpiadora
soap el jabón
soccer el fútbol
soccer ball el balón
socks los calcetines
soda water la soda
somebody alguien
somehow de algún modo
something algo
sometimes a veces
somewhere en alguna parte
son el hijo
song la canción
sorry! ¡perdón!
  I'm sorry perdón/lo siento
  sorry? (pardon) ¿cómo dice?

soup la sopa
south el sur
South America Sudamérica
souvenir el recuerdo
spade la pala
spades (cards) picas
Spain España
Spaniard (man) el español
  (woman) la española
Spanish español
  the Spanish los españoles
speak hablar
  do you speak …? ¿habla …?
  I don't speak … no hablo …
speed la velocidad
speed limit el límite de velocidad
spider la araña
spinach las espinacas
spoon la cuchara
spring (mechanical) el muelle
  (season) la primavera
square (noun: in town) la plaza
  (adj.) cuadrado
staircase la escalera
stairs las escaleras
stamp el sello
stapler la grapadora
star la estrella
start (noun: beginning) el principio
  (verb) empezar
station la estación
statue la estatua
steak el filete
steal robar
  it's been stolen lo han robado
steamer (boat) el vapor
stockings las medias
stomach el estómago
stomachache el dolor de
  estómago
stop (noun: bus) la parada
  (verb) parar
  stop! ¡alto!
storm la tormenta
strawberries las fresas

**stream** *(small river)* el arroyo
**street** la calle
**string** la cuerda
**stroller** la sillita de ruedas
**strong** fuerte
**student** el/la estudiante
**stupid** estúpido
**suburbs** las afueras
**subway** el metro
**sugar** el azúcar
**suit** *(noun)* el traje
  **it suits you** te sienta bien
**suitcase** la maleta
**sun** el sol
**sunbathe** tomar el sol
**sunburn** la quemadura de sol
**sunglasses** las gafas de sol
**sunny: it's sunny** hace sol
**sunshade** la sombrilla
**suntan: to get a suntan**
  broncearse
**suntan lotion** la loción bronceadora
**suntanned** bronceado
**supermarket** el supermercado
**supper** la cena
**supplement** el suplemento
**sure** seguro
**surname** el apellido
**sweat** *(noun)* el sudor
  *(verb)* sudar
**sweater** el jersey
**sweatshirt** la sudadera
**sweet** *(adj.: not sour)* dulce
  *(sherry)* oloroso
**swim** *(verb)* nadar
**swimming pool** la piscina
**swimming trunks** el bañador
**switch** el interruptor
**synagogue** la sinagoga

**table** la mesa
**take** tomar
**take off** el despegue
**talcum powder** los polvos de talco

**talk** *(noun)* la charla
  *(verb)* hablar
**tall** alto
**tampons** los tampones
**tangerine** la mandarina
**tapestry** el tapiz
**tea** el té
**teacher** el profesor
  *(female)* la profesora
**telephone** *(noun)* el teléfono
  *(verb)* llamar por teléfono
**television** la televisión
**temperature** la temperatura
  *(fever)* la fiebre
**tent** la tienda (de campaña)
**tent pole** el mástil
**tent stake** la estaquilla, la estaca
**than** que
**thank** *(verb)* agradecer
  **thank you** gracias
  **thanks** gracias
**that: that one** ése/ésa
  **that bus** ese autobús
  **that man** ese hombre
  **that woman** esa mujer
  **what's that?** ¿qué es eso?
  **I think that …** creo que …
**the** el/la
  *(plural)* los/las *(see p 5)*
**their: their room** su habitación
  **their books** sus libros
  **it's theirs** es suyo
**them: it's for them** es para ellos/ellas
  **give it to them** déselo
**then** entonces
  *(after)* después
**there** allí
  **there is/are …** hay …
  **is/are there …?** ¿hay …?
**these: these men** estos hombres
  **these women** estas mujeres
  **these are mine** éstos son míos
**they** ellos/ellas
**thick** grueso
**thin** delgado

**think** pensar
  **I think so** creo que sí
  **I'll think about it** lo pensaré
**third** tercero
**thirsty: I'm thirsty** tengo sed
**this: this one** éste/ésta
  **this man** este hombre
  **this woman** esta mujer
  **what's this?** ¿qué es esto?
  **this is Mr. ...** éste es el señor ...
**those: those men** esos hombres
  **those women** esas mujeres
**throat** la garganta
**through** por
**thumbtack** la chincheta
**thunderstorm** la tormenta
**ticket** *(train, etc.)* el billete
  *(theater, etc.)* la entrada
**ticket office** la taquilla
**tide** la marea
**tie** *(noun)* la corbata
  *(verb)* atar
**tight** ajustado
**time** tiempo
  **what's the time?** ¿qué hora es?
**timetable** el horario
**tin** hojalata
**tip** *(money)* la propina
  *(end)* la punta
**tire** el neumático
**tired** cansado
**tissues** los pañuelos de papel
**to: to America** a América
  **to the station** a la estación
  **to the doctor** al médico
**toast** la tostada
**tobacco** el tabaco
**today** hoy
**together** juntos
**toilet** *(in a house)* el baño
  *(in public establishment)* los servicos
**toilet paper** el papel higiénico
**tomato** el tomate
**tomato juice** el zumo de tomate
**tomorrow** mañana

**tongue** la lengua
**tonic** la tónica
**tonight** esta noche
**too** *(also)* también
  *(excessively)* demasiado
**tooth** el diente
  **back tooth** la muela
**toothache** el dolor de muelas
**toothbrush** el cepillo de dientes
**toothpaste** la pasta dentífrica
**tour** la excursión
**tourist** el/la turista
**tourist office** la oficina de turismo
**towel** la toalla
**tower** la torre
**town** la ciudad
**town hall** el ayuntamiento
**toy** el juguete
**tractor** el tractor
**tradition** la tradición
**traffic** el tráfico
**traffic jam** el atasco
**traffic lights** el semáforo
**trailer** la caravana, el remolque
**train** el tren
**translate** traducir
**translator** el traductor
  *(female)* la traductora
**travel agency** la agencia de viajes
**traveler's check** el cheque de viaje
**tray** la bandeja
**tree** el árbol
**trip** el viaje
**truck** el camión
**true** cierto
  **it's true** es verdad
**try** intentar
**tunnel** el túnel
**tweezers** las pinzas
**typewriter** la máquina de escribir

**umbrella** el paraguas
**uncle** el tío
**under ...** debajo de ...

141

**underpants** los calzoncillos
**undershirt** la camiseta
**understand** entender
  **I don't understand** no entiendo
**underwear** la ropa interior
**United States** Estados Unidos
**university** la universidad
**unleaded** sin plomo
**until** hasta
**unusual** poco común
**up** arriba
  *(upward)* hacia arriba
**urgent** urgente
**us: it's for us** es para nosotros/nosotras
  **give it to us** dénoslo
**use** *(noun)* el uso
  *(verb)* usar
  **it's no use** no sirve de nada
**useful** útil
**usual** corriente
**usually** en general


**vacancies** *(rooms)* habitaciones libres
**vacation** las vacaciones
**vacuum cleaner** la aspiradora
**valley** el valle
**valve** la válvula
**vanilla** la vainilla
**vase** el jarrón
**veal** la (carne de) ternera
**vegetables** la verdura
**vegetarian** vegetariano
**vehicle** el vehículo
**very** muy
  **very much** mucho
**video** *(tape)* la cinta de vídeo
  *(film)* el vídeo
**video recorder** el (aparato de) vídeo
**view** la vista
**viewfinder** el visor de imagen
**villa** el chalet
**village** el pueblo
**vinegar** el vinagre
**violin** el violín

**visit** *(noun)* la visita
  *(verb)* visitar
**visitor** el/la visitante
**vitamin pills** las vitaminas
**vodka** el vodka
**voice** la voz


**wait** esperar
  **wait!** ¡espere!
**waiter** el camarero
  **waiter!** ¡camarero!
**waiting room** la sala de espera
**waitress** la camarera
  **waitress!** ¡Oiga, por favor!
**Wales** Gales
**walk** *(noun: stroll)* el paseo
  *(verb)* andar
  **to go for a walk** ir de paseo
**wall** la pared
  *(outside)* el muro
**wallet** la cartera
**war** la guerra
**wardrobe** el armario
**warm** caliente
  *(weather)* caluroso
**was** estaba/era
**washing machine** la zapatilla
**wasp** la avispa
**watch** *(noun)* el reloj
  *(verb)* mirar
**water** el agua
**waterfall** la cascada
**water heater** el calentador (de agua)
**wave** *(noun)* la ola
  *(verb)* agitar
**wavy** *(hair)* ondulado
**we** nosotros/nosotras
**weather** el tiempo
**website** la web site, el sitio web
**wedding** la boda
**week** la semana
**welcome** *(verb)* dar la bienvenida
  **you're welcome** no hay de qué
**Welsh** galés

**Welshman** el galés
**Welshwoman** la galesa
**were: we were** éramos/estábamos
  **you were** era/estaba
  *(familiar)* eras/estabas
  **they were** eran/estaban
**west** el oeste
**wet** mojado
**what?** ¿qué?
**wheel** la rueda
**wheelchair** la silla de ruedas
**when?** ¿cuándo?
**where?** ¿dónde?
**whether** si
**which?** ¿cuál?
**whiskey** el whisky
**white** blanco
**who?** ¿quién?
**why?** ¿por qué?
**wide** ancho
  **3 meters wide** de tres metros de anchura
**wife** la mujer
**wind** el viento
**window** la ventana
**wine** el vino
**wine merchant** el vinatero
**wing** el ala
**with** con
**without** sin
**woman** la mujer
**wood** *(material)* la madera
**wool** la lana

**word** la palabra
**work** *(noun)* el trabajo
  *(verb)* trabajar
**worse** peor
**worst** (el) peor
**wrapping paper** el papel de envolver
  *(for presents)* el papel de regalo
**wrench** la llave inglesa
**wrist** la muñeca
**writing paper** el papel de escribir
**wrong** equivocado

**year** el año
**yellow** amarillo
**yes** sí
**yesterday** ayer
**yet** todavía
  **not yet** todavía no
**yogurt** el yogur
**you** usted
  *(familiar)* tú
**your: your book** su libro
  *(familiar)* tu libro
  **your shoes** sus zapatos
  *(familiar)* tus zapatos
**yours: is this yours?** ¿es suyo esto?
  *(familiar)* ¿es tuyo esto?
**youth hostel** el albergue juvenil

**zipper** la cremallera
**zoo** el zoo